"Wow! Jennings and his researchers have taken the complex subject of embracing constant change, reinvention, and growth, and broken it down into simple bite-size pieces. *The Reinventors* will be the catalyst that helps your business achieve its full potential."

> —Dr. Robert Kriegel, *New York Times* bestselling author of *If It Ain't Broke . . . BREAK IT!, Sacred Cows Make the Best Burgers,* and *Performance Under Pressure*

"Leaders of companies like Kodak and Blockbuster should have read Jennings's book on reinvention. Their businesses would surely be more relevant and innovative than they are today. Read this now or take the chance of following their unfortunate fates!"

> —Tommy Spaulding, *New York Times* bestselling author of *It's Not Just Who You Know*

"Jennings's ideas are powerful and highly practical. Embrace the steps he lays out for you in *The Reinventors* and your business will rocket to new heights."

> —Sean Atkins, senior vice president, Discovery Communications, former senior vice president of HBO, and angel investor

"Jason Jennings hits it out of the park with the best road map for change and growth in business today. Read it and reinvent your business like never before!"

> —Mark Thompson, *New York Times* bestselling author of *Success Built to Last,* visiting scholar at Stanford University, and co-founder of Richard Branson's Virgin Unite Growth Academy

"As you read these words your business is either being reinvented or being destroyed. With Jason Jennings's new book, *The Reinventors,* you'll learn how the best leaders conquer this challenge every day and you'll gain a practical blueprint for creating your own success story. I loved this book and you will too."

> —Vince Thompson, author of *Ignited* and managing partner at Middleshift

the
reinventors

How Extraordinary Companies Pursue

Radical Continuous Change

JASON JENNINGS

PORTFOLIO / PENGUIN

PORTFOLIO / PENGUIN
Published by the Penguin Group
Penguin Group (USA) Inc., 375 Hudson Street,
New York, New York 10014, U.S.A.
Penguin Group (Canada), 90 Eglinton Avenue East, Suite 700,
Toronto, Ontario, Canada M4P 2Y3
(a division of Pearson Penguin Canada Inc.)
Penguin Books Ltd, 80 Strand, London WC2R 0RL, England
Penguin Ireland, 25 St Stephen's Green, Dublin 2, Ireland
(a division of Penguin Books Ltd)
Penguin Books Australia Ltd, 250 Camberwell Road, Camberwell,
Victoria 3124, Australia
(a division of Pearson Australia Group Pty Ltd)
Penguin Books India Pvt Ltd, 11 Community Centre, Panchsheel Park,
New Delhi – 110 017, India
Penguin Group (NZ), 67 Apollo Drive, Rosedale, Auckland 0632,
New Zealand (a division of Pearson New Zealand Ltd)
Penguin Books (South Africa) (Pty) Ltd, 24 Sturdee Avenue,
Rosebank, Johannesburg 2196, South Africa

Penguin Books Ltd, Registered Offices:
80 Strand, London WC2R 0RL, England

First published in 2012 by Portfolio / Penguin,
a member of Penguin Group (USA) Inc.

3   5   7   9   10   8   6   4   2

LIBRARY OF CONGRESS CATALOGING-IN-PUBLICATION DATA
Jennings, Jason.
The reinventors : how extraordinary companies pursue radical
continuous change / Jason Jennings.
p. cm.
Includes index.
ISBN 978-1-59184-423-5
1. Total quality management.   I. Title.
HD62.15.J46 2012
658.4'06—dc23
2012005774

Printed in the United States of America
Set in Bembo with Friz Quadrata
Designed by Sabrina Bowers

ALWAYS LEARNING   PEARSON

*To Bruce Ritter, longtime friend and financial adviser,
who came up with the idea for this book*

CONTENTS

the
reinventors

INTRODUCTION

I broke Thomas Wolfe's cardinal rule and went back home to the town where I grew up. I parked my rental car a block off Main Street intending to wander through the downtown business district.

I remember it being filled with bustling department and clothing stores, drugstores, restaurants, more barbershops and salons than you could count, crowded supermarkets, hardware centers, and insurance agencies. It was so jammed with cars and people, you had to look both ways before you stepped off the curb to avoid being run over.

But as I turned the corner, I saw a ghost town minus the tumbleweeds.

Boarded-up buildings were covered with grime and graffiti, parking meters were mere stumps, their heads lopped off in hopes that saving a quarter would cause shoppers to return, and there wasn't anyplace to buy anything. The only things left were a few little bars and a handful of antique and junk stores.

As I walked, memories of the people I knew who had owned and operated the stores that lined the streets came flooding back. There were the Lowenstein sisters, who had owned the town's flagship department store. Leah, Rose, and Bertha had fought successfully, like Patton battled the Germans, to keep competitors from gaining ground on their turf, and often swatted competitors away with the phrase "There are already enough stores downtown and we don't need any more!"

There was the town's favorite drugstore owner, Joe, who when asked if he was planning on building a new store out on the highway where some out-of-towners were constructing new stores had replied, "No way, they're all going to go belly-up because nobody's going to drive all the way to the highway to shop." For the record, the highway is five *blocks* from downtown and has become the main shopping area.

I also heard the voice of Tony the barber, whom I'd once asked if he wanted to grow his business and get bigger and who'd replied, "I don't want any more business and I don't want to grow. I'm happy with things just the way they are."

I had liked and respected these people. They were businesspeople—successful, smart, sophisticated, and I'd grown up thinking they must have known something and must have had most of the right answers or they wouldn't have been running a business.

During my trip home I asked around and heard the depressing last chapters of the Lowenstein sisters, our family druggist, the affable Tony, and all their peers. Not *one* of the downtown merchants had ever gotten a dime from the sale of their business. In fact, as the tsunami of regional malls, discount centers, outlet malls, rapidly changing shopping patterns, the Internet, and shopping on our smartphones chipped away at their business, it was death by a thousand cuts. They were too old, too tired, too set in their ways, or too entitled to ever change anything, and they remained stubborn in their belief that because they were *there* they had a right to be successful. One by one their businesses spiraled into closure.

It would be easy to write these people off as small-town simpletons or remnants of a world that no longer exists. But when you read between the lines these people are like a lot of us. The Lowenstein sisters focused on the competition instead of the customer. Joe the druggist had all the answers. And Tony's business wasn't broke, so why should he mess with it? It's all very familiar.

My hometown is an apt metaphor for what will happen to you, your job, and your business unless you become a reinventor completely committed to constant radical change and growth.

EVERYONE MUST BECOME
A REINVENTOR

Your job as you know it and your business as it is currently run will eventually change. The only chance any of us have for prosperity is to constantly reimagine, rethink, and reinvent everything we do and how we do it in order to remain relevant. We must all become reinventors, and we'd better do it quickly.

Compare the list of the top twenty-five companies in the Fortune 500 in the year 2000 and the year 2010. The results are shocking. Sixteen of the top twenty-five companies fell off their lofty perches in the span of only ten years. That's almost two-thirds!

Dig a little deeper and you'll find that since the Fortune 500 list was first published in 1955 more than 90 percent of the companies on it have been mopped up by smaller rivals, gone bankrupt, shrunk so small that they have become inconsequential, or simply closed their doors.

These companies were once the largest and most stable businesses in the nation. Certainly these thriving organizations had the intellectual and financial resources to ensure their continued success. Amoco got merged away; Esmark was acquired by Beatrice Foods, which later got sopped up by ConAgra; Armour got split up into parts; Navistar was delisted from the NYSE; Union Carbide was swallowed by Dow; and Firestone ended up sold to Japanese interests. Only one company, DuPont, has appeared on every Fortune 500 list.

All of these companies failed to constantly evolve, change, grow, and reinvent themselves, and eventually they were kicked to the curb.

Today, a combination of stagnant Western markets, former third world nations embracing technology and becoming manufacturing powerhouses with middle classes larger than that of the U.S., technology that makes everything increasingly transparent, and customers who believe that they can get exactly what they want when they want it at a price they're willing to pay all add up to a game-changing business environment. Anyone who thinks that they'll get a free pass and that they don't have to constantly reinvent their business has their head in the sand.

HOW *THE REINVENTORS* CAME TO BE

As part of my preparation for teaching and speeches, I conduct about eight hundred telephone interviews annually with business owners, senior leaders, executives, and CEOs. Two questions I ask each of them are, "What's keeping you awake at night about business?" and "What are the stumbling blocks or challenges that could get in the way of your business achieving its full economic potential?"

As the Great Recession of 2007–2009 came to a close, people stopped talking only about staying alive and started responding with their concerns about the need to reinvent their business models.

While considering the possibility of doing a book on the subject, I received a call from a friend attending a conference that helped me decide to pull the pin. He's not normally a very excitable guy, but he was almost out of breath when I answered his call. "You're not going to believe some numbers I just heard," he said, "and if nothing else convinces you to do the book on reinvention, they will."

The startling numbers he was referring to were from the 2010 IBM Global CEO Study. It turns out that 67 percent of worldwide CEOs think their current business model is only sustainable for another three years, while another 31 percent believe their current model might have as long as five years.

Between everyone I was interviewing talking about their need to reinvent themselves and their companies and 98 percent of global CEOs believing their current business models were ultimately unsustainable, I decided to learn as much as I could about reinvention.

THE RESEARCH

In the spirit of becoming a reinventor, I changed the ways I used to research previous books, outsourcing the task of helping me identify the people and companies who've done the best job of reinventing their businesses and reducing the research time by two-thirds.

Initial research yielded more than twenty-two thousand stories, articles, and blogs published in the past ten years with the key words *reinvention*, *reinvent*, and *reinventor*. By reviewing the first few paragraphs of each article we were able to discard almost 90 percent of them because of either age (too old), size (too small), or repetition. Most of our rejections were due to the zealous misuse and overuse of the word *reinvention*.

I studied the remaining several thousand stories in search of the one hundred most compelling examples of reinvention by asking the following questions: Has the company truly demonstrated a significant reinvention? Is it doing well financially with a seemingly bright future? Will it be an interesting company to study? Is it of a size that both entrepreneurs and leaders of large organizations could learn from? Am I likely to learn something I don't already know? Next came interviews with the companies in an effort to identify the most compelling cases for reinvention, followed by field research and interviews with people at all levels of the organizations. From the one hundred, I selected the best examples of companies who successfully embraced continuous change for inclusion in the book.

A SURPRISING FINDING

I undertook this project with the vague notion that reinvention was about moving a business from point A to point B. But that's not what I found. We discovered that in the process of moving from A to B these businesses developed new skill sets and values that allowed them to quickly progress to C, D, E, and beyond.

They all became serial reinventors and embraced constant radical change.

Good business is about making certain you're providing something of value to someone willing to pay you enough to make it worth your while. Reinventors make certain they're *continually* providing something of value to someone willing to pay them enough to make it worthwhile.

This book isn't about outsourcing, and it won't tell you where to build your factories, how to distribute your goods or services, who your customers will be, what your business model will look like, or even what business you'll be in. But it will teach you how to figure out all those things on your own and provide you with lessons and principles to give you a head start on everyone else.

You're about to learn what people and companies who continually reinvent themselves and their organizations do to stay ahead. If you're ready, this book will help you and your business become a serial reinventor.

CHAPTER 1

CONSTANT CHANGE AND GROWTH

Companies committed to growth make staying ahead of their customers' wants and needs a hallmark of their culture and accomplish that goal through constant radical change and reinvention.

S everal years ago I was standing in front of an audience of highly accomplished engineers and executives at an electronics company. I wanted to help them get their heads around the topic I was about to address, so I asked three questions.

"How many of you would like to earn more money?"

Every hand went up, including those of the newly hired recruits; low, mid-level, and senior executives; and even the C-suite senior executives.

"Now, raise your hand again if you hope that someday you'll receive a promotion or have more responsibility."

Once again, it was unanimous; every hand reached high into the air.

Then, I asked my final question: "And when would you like to begin earning more money and having more responsibility—sooner, or later?"

Accompanied by big smiles, "SOONER!" echoed loudly throughout the room.

As I glanced at the CEO, it appeared he'd heard something he didn't like. At the break I asked if something was wrong. "No, not wrong," he said, "but those questions you asked are going to keep me up tonight. They all want to grow and do better, and I'd better not let them down."

He was more right than he knew.

Since then I've asked that question of nearly a half million people who have attended my speeches, and having witnessed the same number of hands in the air it seems fair to conclude that wanting to improve one's financial condition and achieve one's full potential are universal desires.

Buried in the shared hopes of workers are two mammoth problems with huge consequences for the owners and leaders of businesses of every size and that speak directly to the need for constant radical change and reinvention:

▶ If a business isn't growing, the people who want to make more money and have more responsibility won't get what they want when they want it, and they'll find a reason to leave and pursue better opportunities elsewhere.

▶ Unless a business is constantly undergoing radical change, it will never be able to stay ahead of its customers' constantly changing wants and needs, and its growth will first falter and then completely stop.

Two of the primary responsibilities of a business leader are to keep a highly motivated team of people together and to make certain the team stays ahead of a growing base of customers who have constantly changing wants and needs. Everything else can be dealt with and managed.

There's *never* been a business that has reached a desired level of revenues or profits and then remained static or stayed at the same level for any significant length of time. Even those that make it to the top of the Fortune 1000 are on a slippery slope. Two out of three were able to hold their ground from 1973 to 1983, but from 1993 to 2003 almost two out of three were leaders no more. It's not going to get any easier to stay at the top in the future.

Every business must be constantly and quickly changing, growing, and moving forward or they'll eventually find themselves in a downward spiral that will ultimately result in their demise. Stalled companies historically lose almost 75 percent of their market value and often see their CEO and senior team kicked to the curb. Their replacements get saddled with long odds against them. Not even one out of two stalled companies find their way back to a healthy (4 percent or more) top line growth.

CONVENTIONAL WISDOM WON'T PROVIDE CONTINUAL GROWTH

Achieving and sustaining healthy growth is the biggest single challenge that every business will face during each day of its existence, because consistent growth simply isn't common, and profitable growth is even rarer. While studying companies around the globe, Bain and Company Research found that nine out of ten businesses routinely fail to earn the cost of the capital invested in them. In fact, average annual growth in the 1990s was 1.4 percent, and it was even less in the 2000s.

The research for my book *Think Big, Act Small* bolsters the findings of Bain and Company Research. Despite spending two years studying more than seventy-two thousand companies around the world, my research team and I were able to identify only 120 businesses that had achieved double-digit organic growth for ten consecutive years.

TIRED OLD EXCUSES FOR LITTLE OR NO GROWTH

Instead of accepting personal responsibility and addressing the root cause—an unwillingness to embrace radical change—for their lack of growth, many business leaders spend their time finding excuses for their poor performance. Their questionable explanations get retold so frequently by so many that they receive de facto validation. Here are some examples of the most used excuses:

▶ **"It's the economy; we'll get better when times get better."** Margins, return on assets, and top line growth have declined consistently over the past four decades. Those years have seen seven recessions and seven recoveries. More of the same should be expected. Recessions are actually a great time to grow; more than half of today's members of the Dow Jones Industrial Average opened their doors and began prospering during recessions.

▶ **"Slow growth is outside our control."** Acts of God, recessions, antitrust policies, Republican or Democratic administrations—uncontrollable events are responsible for less than one out of every five stalls in business. Eighty-three percent of companies are doomed by unforced errors in execution. We'll discuss other internal, controllable issues in upcoming chapters.

▶ **"We can't grow because we're too big (or too old)."** To be sure, it's not the big that eat the small; it's the fast that eat the slow. But since I first penned that attack on conventional wisdom in 2000, many large organizations have blown up their bureaucratic speed bumps and remade themselves to think big but act small. And it's not just big technology companies who've radically changed; smokestack businesses, distribution, retail, even education companies have proven any business can grow.

▶ **"Cost cutting is our key to growth."** Even though strategies to accomplish more with less have time and time again spurred incredible innovation and growth, old-fashioned, share-the-pain, across-the-board cost cutting has failed to create profitable growers 93 percent of the time. Why? Because pruning 10 or 15 percent from all parts of a business still leaves you spending 85 percent on activities that don't contribute and cutting precious investment dollars from your best opportunities for a big payback. This is called feeding the weeds while starving the flowers.

▶ **"Acquisitions are our key to growth."** We can all remember good examples, such as when eBay bought PayPal and Disney bought Pixar. Or the decade when IBM hit scores of home runs and ran up their revenues 50 percent and Cisco added $8.8 billion in sales through buying and growing other companies. There are notable examples of game-changing acquisitions that propelled organizations to double-digit growth. But as the adage says, " 'For example' is not proof." Acquisitions are minefields with booby traps everywhere. Nearly two-thirds of merged companies get trapped and stall within a quarter after announcing an acquisition, and almost 90 percent of companies fail to accelerate growth significantly in the following three years, according to research firm McKinsey Global Institute.

▶ **"People are unwilling or unable to change."** When Bob Nardelli rolled out his sweeping plan to reinvent the Home Depot, he didn't get a lot of buy-in. "There's no way I was going to be part of Bob's [*bleeping*] Army," one executive confided. But many of those same executives went on to management positions at other big-box organizations and did very well. They changed, just not for Nardelli. Research shows that only one out of five people have such deep-seated issues with any change. The majority, 63 percent, will pitch in and help you reinvent as soon as they believe it is safe and the end result has a good chance of succeeding. (The remaining 17 percent are your early adopters—they're ready to reinvent when you say "Go.")

BUILDING A CULTURE OF CHANGE AND GROWTH

One of the most important decisions a leader will make is to determine what kind of culture the organization should have. The hardest nonstop work they'll ever do is to live the culture (and be seen as living it) and to get and keep everyone on board the same culture bandwagon.

Culture is defined as the shared attitudes, values, goals, and practices of an organization; every group of people has a culture. Whether it's a small restaurant, a medium-size office, or a multinational corporation with a hundred thousand employees, each group has a distinct culture, either the culture desired by the leadership and the one they constantly strive to spread throughout the organization or the one that exists by default.

When a leader fails to provide the proper culture, one will still exist; it can best be described as one of every man for himself, each acting in his own best interests and to heck with the interests of the company.

One of the best examples of a company that has created a culture of growth and embraced constant change and reinvention, where everyone is aware of the culture, is Apollo Tyres, of India. The company does business in India, where it has a network of more than four thousand retailers who sell its products, in South Africa, where it has nearly one thousand dealerships, and in the Netherlands.

By 2005, Apollo had spent several decades becoming a small, respected manufacturer of tires in the Indian marketplace. According to the company's young managing director, Neeraj Kanwar, "We found ourselves in the same position that many other companies do. We were doing three hundred million dollars a year in revenue, constantly fighting fires and spending all our time on things that probably weren't the best use of our time."

Kanwar likens the company's position at the time to an old-fashioned phonograph. "The record on the turntable kept going round and round but the needle was stuck. Some years," he says, "we'd be up a few percent in revenues, and the next year down a couple percent, and we kept repeating that over and over again." The breakthrough that caused Apollo to embrace constant growth and the change required to achieve it occurred in 2005.

"We had a meeting of the top twenty people in the company," Kanwar says, "and for the first time seriously asked ourselves where we were, where we were headed, and where we wanted to go. Until that point," he says, "what was missing was having a big goal."

During a retreat away from company headquarters the group decided they wanted to grow the company more than sixfold, to two billion dollars, in the following five years, which would put them among the top fifteen tire companies in the world.

"Once we knew what our big objective was, we were totally committed to growth," says the U.S.-educated Kanwar. "The next obvious step was to ask ourselves what we'd need to do to make it happen."

The group decided they could drive the company to two billion dollars in annual revenues within their ambitious five-year time frame if they adhered to three principles, which became known as the Apollo Pillars: people, technology, and quality.

"On the people front, we were united," says Kanwar, "and decided the more the merrier. We needed more talent, and the talent we had needed more training, because they were the primary asset that would get us to two billion dollars. One of our immediate changes," he says, "was the launch of our Apollo Laureate Academy, designed to train everyone from our senior leadership down to people on the shop floor. We totally reinvented how we find, keep, and grow people." This was the first pillar.

For the second pillar, "we made a complete commitment to technology on every front," says Kanwar. "Making applied technology available to everyone within the company not only made their lives easier but makes decision making a snap and allows for nonstop reinvention to happen.

"When we refer to quality being the third pillar of our journey, you might think I'm referring to the quality of our products," says Kanwar, "but I'm not. Having the highest-quality product goes without saying. Instead, we made a commitment to quality in *every* single thing we do and undertake at every level of the company. One of our aspirations is to win the coveted Deming Prize for quality."

There was an unspoken fourth pillar in the Apollo growth and reinvention journey: speed. "My philosophy," says Kanwar, "is that if something is worth doing it's worth doing as fast as possible. It's not natural to do things slowly," he says. "If you've made up your mind, just do it and get it done.

"Once you've made a commitment to constant growth and you've gotten everyone on board and you've agreed on the principles that will guide your journey, the things that need to be reinvented become obvious," adds Kanwar, completing his thought with a profound "Reinvention isn't something you do once or twice or now and then. It's something you do on a daily basis, and leading a business that embraces constant radical change is a lot more fun than listening to a phonograph with a stuck needle."

If a leader truly wants to build a business committed to growth and change, then that message must become a vital part of the culture, and everyone must know it and practice it.

A CULTURE OF CHANGE AND GROWTH MEANS A BETTER TOMORROW FOR EVERYONE

When a business is growing quickly, all the stakeholders—workers, leaders, customers, suppliers, and investors—are happy and reap financial rewards. When a business isn't growing, those same stakeholders begin to suffer financially, imagine darker tomorrows looming on the horizon, and eventually start looking elsewhere for better opportunities.

Workers

Abraham Maslow nailed it in his landmark work *Hierarchy of Needs: A Theory of Human Motivation*.

Nobody woke up this morning and said, "I sure hope tomorrow sucks more than today." The human condition is to hope for a better tomorrow and to always improve one's circumstances in life. When someone joins a company she's making a bet. She's counting on continued employment, pay raises, developing new skills, being promoted, and eventually being able to achieve a better life for herself and her family and to gain some sense of financial security.

Once a worker's needs for food, clothing, and shelter are fulfilled he begins striving for self-esteem, achievement, the respect of others around him, creativity, spontaneity, and problem solving. Unless a business is growing, there's no opportunity for a worker to grow and achieve those things, and he will start searching for fulfillment elsewhere. Howard Schultz, founder and CEO of Starbucks, realizes that and included growth platforms in his new seven-point transformation agenda for the company. "You can't attract and retain great people for a company that isn't going to grow," he says. "We have to instill a deep sense of commitment to growing the company."

Eventually, unless a company is changing and growing, wages get frozen, downsizing occurs, layoffs take place, and the company ends up with a disappointed, disillusioned, and cynical workforce. Sooner or later the most promising and talented workers leave because they can't see a future that will allow them to achieve their full potential; following their departure, all that generally remains is a group of unskilled, unmotivated, directionless people who merely go through the motions and are unemployable anywhere else.

When a company is constantly changing and its revenues and profits are growing—assuming the ownership and leadership have learned the lesson that wealth must be shared with the people responsible for creating it—you'll more than likely find a happy and highly engaged workforce.

Customers

Customers are a smart bunch of people and know a lot more than most companies realize.

Last year I went holiday shopping at an upscale mall located in an affluent suburb of San Francisco. One of the mall's anchor tenants is a store owned by Federated Department Stores, the nation's largest chain of department stores. As I walked through the store I had a strange feeling of déjà vu, of having experienced the exact same shopping experience at another time in the past. I stopped, looked around, and realized I'd *had* the precise experience before.

At that same moment a woman, who must have been reading my mind, said, "It's so sad, isn't it?"

"Excuse me?" I said.

"The decorations," she replied. "I saw you looking at them. They haven't changed them for years." She concluded as she walked away, "It used to be such a beautiful and busy store."

I looked closer, and sure enough, all the decorations in the store were the same ones I remembered from the last time I'd been there, several holiday seasons before. The trees, the fake gift boxes underneath them, and the artificial poinsettias showed a lot of wear and tear and even dust. The tired old decorations spoke volumes, and I instinctively felt bad for the store and its employees. Like the woman who had spoken to me, I concluded the company must not be doing very well financially, or else it would have money to invest in new merchandising.

As soon as I was able to get online I checked the company's five-year financial performance and discovered its 2010 sales were barely what they'd been five years before, and their profits were less than a quarter of what they'd been back then. When the money coming in the door isn't always increasing, there's no money to plow back into the business, which often signals the start of a downward spiral.

Customers, knowingly or not, seek an experience to accompany the product or service they're purchasing, and the business that offers the best experience in that category wins.

Any business that wants to keep and grow its customers must have constant revenue and profit growth to guarantee having sufficient capital available to fund future growth, and to be able to continue ratcheting up a constantly improving business experience.

When a company is constantly changing, with revenues and profits consistently growing and a piece of the profits being plowed back into the business to further improve the shopping and buying experience, you'll likely find engaged customers waiting for the next opportunity to spend money.

Vendors and Suppliers

All customers are not created equal.

When a company is growing, the vendors and suppliers with whom it does business are also able to grow and see a brighter future for themselves. It's only fair that the vendors and suppliers in turn bestow favored status on companies that pay their bills, treat them well, and increase the amount of money they spend, and where they see potential for even more revenue growth.

There's a company based in New York that's been selling floor coverings for almost a hundred years. From humble beginnings selling carpeting to homeowners, the firm has successfully reinvented itself many times over and today operates globally, specializing in providing all types of flooring surfaces for multiple high-traffic environments in the retail, hospitality, and food-service areas. I'll never forget a conversation I had with the firm's CEO a few years ago that truly enlightened me about how companies view their customers.

In confidence he mentioned one national chain that had been his customer for years. He gave a single thumb down and said, "They aren't opening any stores this year, they're not spending any money with anybody, and they won't be around for long." Then he added, "Their concept has run the course." When speaking about another customer, he said, "They're great to deal with and we bend over backward for them. They're growing like crazy and they treat their suppliers like human beings." Finally, about the well-known chain Circuit City, which did go bankrupt during the most recent recession, he offered two thumbs down and said, "They're total jerks, and all their suppliers are in a betting pool to see how long it is before they go upside down. I've got a hundred bucks on them failing within the next couple of years."

One might question the wisdom of the head of a company forecasting the imminent demise of some of his customers, but the fact is we're all human. We all have opinions, and we all share them with others. One good way to avoid having your vendors and suppliers put the hex on your future and to guarantee that you receive positive buzz is to make certain you're growing and that everyone knows it.

When a business stops growing it frequently turns to treating its vendors and suppliers poorly, constantly squeezing them on price in order to temporarily maintain its profit margins, delaying payments to momentarily bolster cash flow, and playing one supplier against another. A gloomy future is preordained when that conduct becomes a company's way of doing business.

When a company is growing it is more likely to acknowledge the importance of its vendors and suppliers and treat them fairly. In return, its suppliers frequently become trusted partners in uncovering new business opportunities. When a company is constantly changing and its revenues and profits are growing you'll generally find a more engaged group of vendors and suppliers who are interested in truly being good business partners.

Investors/Shareholders

Every business has shareholders or investors, who justly expect a payoff from their investment.

If a company is publicly traded, then its shareholders demand either dividends or sufficient growth in the share price to justify their continued investment. If that doesn't happen, they lose interest and move on, looking for other places to invest their money. There's seldom a second chance with smart money.

Most privately owned businesses have lines of credit or other borrowings from financial institutions, which require the regular submission of financial data. When a lender sees growth, it's likely to continue to provide and increase funding. When there isn't a consistent track record of growth it starts becoming concerned about getting paid back and quickly resorts to decreasing lines of credit, accelerating payment terms, calling notes due, and taking what lenders refer to as an "active interest" in the business, which translates to the lender telling the owners and managers how it wants the business run. The implied threat is always, "Do what we tell you to do or we'll shut you down."

Even sole proprietorships have an investor, and that's the business owner. She's the person who risked it all on an idea she believed in and worked long and hard to make it a reality. She is worthy of a payoff, but without constant growth in revenues and profits it won't happen.

When a company is constantly changing and keeping the market on the edge of its seat wondering what is coming next, and when its revenues and profits are growing consistently, you'll generally find a happy group of investors and lenders fully prepared to help take the business to the next level.

All the Other Stakeholders

There are loads of other stakeholders whose ultimate success is dependent on continued revenue and profit growth.

Unless the business is constantly growing, there won't be money to fund your better tomorrow. Financial peace of mind, solid savings for retirement, paid mortgages, good schools for the children, vacations, and a few toys along the way occur only if a business grows and prospers.

Most people's circles of friends are dominated by business connections and people with whom they've worked or done business. When you're doing well, your friendships do well, and friends and colleagues help lead you to even more opportunities. Sadly, when your business isn't growing or doing well, either you don't have time for friends or they don't have time for you. If your business fails, many friends drift away, almost as if they're afraid of catching whatever you caught.

Charitable, civic, and religious organizations are stakeholders too, and they rely on the generosity of growing businesses to support their good works. If a company isn't growing, it is unable to fund the important work of those institutions.

MAKING A COMMITMENT TO CONSTANT RADICAL CHANGE AND GROWTH

Highly successful companies that grow consistently adhere to the following guiding principles:

▶ Businesses exist to grow revenues and profits.

▶ They are committed to keeping, growing, and rewarding the right people.

▶ They grow by finding, keeping, and growing more customers.

▶ Finding, keeping, and growing more customers occurs as a result of staying ahead of those customers' continually changing wants and needs.

▶ Staying ahead of customers requires constant radical change and reinvention.

The faster a company makes those things happen the happier everyone will be, and the longer the good times will continue.

Ready?

If you agree with the preceding guiding principles, then you're ready to begin engaging in constant radical change and reinvention. But first, you need to let go of a few things. Read on.

CONSTANT CHANGE AND GROWTH: ACTION PLAN

▶ If a business isn't growing between 5 and 10 percent annually, the good, highly talented people won't get the responsibility and the financial rewards they want, and they'll leave.

▶ Unless a business embraces constant change, it won't be able to stay ahead of its customers' constantly changing wants and needs.

▶ Change and reinvention are intentional and don't happen magically. Embracing change and reinvention must be vital components of the organization's culture.

▶ A business needs a set of principles to guide growth and reinvention.

▶ The old excuses that a lack of growth is because of the economy, because of the size or age of the business, or outside the control of the company demonstrate a complete lack of leadership.

▶ When growth stalls, companies lose as much as 75 percent of their market value, and not even one out of two find their way back to a healthy (4 percent or more) top line growth.

▶ Constant growth is required to fulfill the needs of all the stakeholders: the workers, the customers, the vendors and suppliers, the shareholders, and the community. According to Bain and Company Research, nine out of ten businesses routinely fail to earn the cost of the capital invested in them, and 1.4 percent annual growth was the average for all businesses in the 1990s and even less in the 2000s.

CHAPTER 2

LETTING GO

Before you can implement radical change, you have to let go of the things that will destine your attempts for failure, and make letting go a vital part of your culture.

As a pioneer in an industry that conceals its manufacturing strategies as if they were atomic secrets, Ford was astonished to get Toyota's invitation.

"We invite you to visit our newest manufacturing plant," the invitation read. "Send your top engineers and bring all your questions. We're anxious to share our methods." Many senior executives at Ford thought it all sounded too good to be true.

When the engineers returned from their visit to Japan they agreed that the skeptics had been right. "It wasn't a *real* auto manufacturing facility," plant engineers explained. "Sure they had chassis and tools and people, but spare parts and components were virtually nonexistent." The warehouse was too small to support the level of scheduled activity. "It was staged," they concluded, "like a movie."

The truth, as Massachusetts Institute of Technology senior lecturer Dr. C. Otto Scharmer wrote in his book *Theory U, Leading from the Future as It Emerges*, was that nothing had been staged.

What the experts from Ford witnessed was indeed the real deal, the incredibly lean manufacturing system, the *kaizen*—a Japanese word that means continuous improvement—breakthroughs that were about to propel Toyota to the world's number one automaker, while

Detroit's big three automakers began a market-share free fall that tumbled from more than 90 percent to less than 40 percent today.

How did all of those brilliant minds from Ford miss what was right before their eyes? They went to Japan with a detailed picture of the proper setup of an assembly line and a firm understanding, gained though advanced degrees and years of big-time experience, of the rules that governed the world of twentieth-century manufacturing. That was their Achilles' heel.

Innovator Charles Kettering, the longtime head of research at General Motors and a prolific inventor, had warned his industry colleagues about getting caught in this trap. "An inventor is simply a fellow who doesn't take his education too seriously," he said. In other words, inventors are engineers who can let go of their expertness and achieve what Apple's late CEO, Steve Jobs, called the "lightness of being a beginner again."

Before you can begin to embrace and implement continuous radical change and reinvention, you and/or your business have to let go of the reinvention killers that will destine your attempts for failure.

LETTING GO IS HARD TO DO

The following story illustrates just how difficult letting go can be.

Certain parts of the world, especially India and parts of Asia, have a real problem with troops of. marauding monkeys. These critters steal food, destroy crops, and are even responsible for having transmitted the HIV virus to the human population. When monkeys move from being a mere nuisance to being a full-blown threat, they have to be captured and moved.

The most common method of catching monkeys has been to

shoot them with tranquilizer guns, place them in crates, and move them to the wild. But monkeys are very fragile creatures, and many of them die as a result of being captured this way. In recent years animal rights activists have forced monkey catchers to revert to a method of capture that's hundreds of years old. Here's how it works.

Enlightened monkey catchers use only a bag of gourds, some string, a sharp knife, and peanuts or candy to handily capture their unsuspecting victims.

Upon spotting a group of monkeys in a tree, the monkey catcher begins by tossing a few small stones or pieces of bark into the tree to scatter and isolate them. Then, moving to the base of a tree where a monkey is perched, he takes out one of the gourds, cuts it in half, hollows it out, puts the two pieces back together, and wraps it round and round with string.

Using his knife, he cuts a small hole in the gourd, and then, in full view of the monkey, he begins stuffing the gourd with candy or nuts. Very curious by nature, the monkey watches intently as the monkey catcher continues filling the gourd with treats.

When the gourd is about half-full, the monkey catcher sets it down on the ground and backs off. Sensing an opportunity, the monkey quickly scrambles down from the tree, grabs the gourd, tries to peer inside, smells something it wants, and begins working its tiny hand through the tinier hole in hot pursuit of what's inside.

Wrestling its hand deep into the gourd, the monkey grabs a handful of treats. However, when it tries to remove its prize-filled fist from the gourd, it can't get it out. The harder it tries, the less success it has, and eventually the monkey catcher approaches the preoccupied monkey, delivers a quick shot of a short-term tranquilizer, and places the monkey in a crate for its journey to a new home.

The moral of the story is best posed as a question: What was the only thing the monkey had to do to get free?

The answer, of course, is "Let go."

But it's simply not in a monkey's DNA to let go when its little fist is stuffed with candy or nuts.

"Hey, I'm no chimp," you might say. No, of course you're not. We humans only share 98.5 percent of our DNA with monkeys. I'm guessing that the gene for not letting go is part of the DNA we have in common.

SMOKE JUMPERS SHARE THAT GENE

Smoke jumpers are highly trained, highly evolved elite firefighters who parachute into difficult terrain to put out wildfires. They need to have an extensive résumé in remote terrain firefighting and be skilled in using the tools of the trade. They must be in excellent physical condition and possess a high degree of emotional stability and mental alertness.

In the middle of the past century, fifteen of the bravest smoke jumpers were battling in a deep canyon when suddenly the inferno turned and raced right at them. The men tried to retreat, scrambling up the steep walls to get away. Tragically, twelve souls were lost; only three were able to escape.

The testimony of the three survivors and a review of the scene revealed a surprising finding. Large poleaxes, shovels, and twelve heavy backpacks, in all some 115 pounds per man of professional gear, were on the ground hundreds of yards from where the smoke jumpers first turned from fighting the wildfire to race away. Only three dropped their gear early; the rest couldn't let go until it was too late.

In *Linking Expertise and Naturalistic Decision Making*, research psychologist Gary Klein explains that this is all too human. Those tools represented who they were as men. Dropping them was like abandoning their knowledge and relationships for uncertainty. It was a hard choice to make, and sadly, the majority of them will never have a second chance to learn how to make the right choice in the future.

The same is true of you, me, and all of us. When we've got something we want in our tightly clenched hands, we'll resist like hell before letting it go.

It's not possible to embrace change and reinvent a business until you're able to let go of the eight following reinvention killers.

THE REINVENTION KILLERS

Yesterday's Breadwinners

Every product or service has a natural life cycle that begins with an introduction, followed by growth, maturity, and inevitably a decline as it becomes yesterday's breadwinner. There are no exceptions.

The bulk of revenues and profits of any service or product is generated during the growth and maturity phases. By the time a product, service, or process has entered the phase of its natural decline, it should ideally have already been replaced with something more lucrative.

One would imagine that any highly intelligent business leader would be quick to offload its crumb bearers, but business history repeatedly demonstrates that even the best companies—much like the smoke jumpers—find it very hard to let go of what they see as their legacy services and products, and frequently hold on to them so long they end up destroying the enterprise.

Almost thirty years ago the leadership of Eastman Kodak was

warned by its own engineers that one day digital photography would replace film. The company couldn't let go and continued unprofitably producing and selling film while enduring countless rounds of layoffs and downsizing, managing to stay alive only by the benefit of proceeds from lawsuits against other companies. It couldn't let go of a legacy product.

In another example, several of the world's big music companies, such as Universal Music Group, BMG, and EMI, could have easily opened the world's first online music store separately or together, but each refused to let go of a business model that had allowed them to enrich themselves and abuse artists, distributors, and broadcasters for decades. Instead, they continued to fight constant court battles to ensure that things would remain as they'd always been. Then along came Apple—a computer company—which used the iPod and iTunes to knock the old music companies to the mat; they never got back up. They couldn't let go of a very old business model, while Apple quickly proceeded to sell ten billion songs to its more than one hundred million customers in just a few years.

The now bankrupt Blockbuster could have easily used its vast resources to build a side-by-side business distributing DVDs by mail, but the company couldn't let go of its lucrative model of forcing people to drive to its inconvenient, cheap rental locations and actually took pleasure in charging customers late fees (which made up most of its profits), so upstart Netflix did it instead and put the first nail in Blockbuster's coffin. A few years later, Redbox began placing thousands of convenient kiosks across the nation, charging people a dollar a day for a movie rental. Within two years the company was doing more than six hundred million rentals annually, all but ensuring Blockbuster's near total demise. With a handful of stores remaining, Blockbuster was merely a shadow of its former self. Blockbuster couldn't let go of wanting things to be the way they'd always been.

AOL, which at one time had thirty million users and a market capitalization of almost three hundred billion dollars and ended up buying Time Warner, couldn't let go of dial-up access and is now a mere shadow of its former self, with a couple million customers. It is desperately trying to reinvent itself but probably doesn't have the capital to pull it off. The company arrogantly refused to let go of its business model, even though it had known years earlier that one day soon blazingly fast Internet speeds would render its service irrelevant.

"Great companies [inevitably] develop a rowboat mentality," says Sir Howard Stringer, chairman and CEO of Sony. They are "always looking behind to past successes" with awe and admiration as they row into the future. Stringer saw that rowboat mind-set firsthand when he took over at Sony six years ago. "We were very comfortable making analog boxes [such as the phenomenally successful Walkman]," he says. Success had made Sony "slow" and caused the company to "miss critical technology transitions," which hurt profit margins and gave competitors an opportunity to eat Sony's lunch. (Apple had sold thirty million iPods by the time Stringer took charge in 2005, and the next year sold another forty-six million units.) Stringer quickly initiated an effort to let go of yesterday's breadwinners (like the Walkman line) and lose the rowboat mind-set. "We are working hard to avoid living in our past," he says. Stringer recognized that the real culprit standing in the way of progress at Sony was a tradition-bound mentality and began systematically letting go of the traditions and people that had hamstrung the company.

Military leaders are notorious for clinging to the successful tactics of the past when creating a strategy for achieving victory. Winston Churchill, the revered former prime minister of England and one of the greatest military minds of all time, understood this failing but feared that his irascible, larger-than-life personality and the yes-men who surround all leaders might keep him from thinking differently and changing tactics to fit a changing battlefield. So he hired a group of six number crunchers, gave them direct access, and demanded they present him with a steady stream of facts and data—honest, unfiltered, and without concern for those who would be offended by his saying, "I have no need for cheering dreams to help me sleep. Facts are better than dreams."

Yesterday's breadwinners are a lot like the tactics that won the last war. They won't help you succeed. Like Churchill, you need facts and data to reinvent. The most important is the data that helps you understand your customer.

Recently it was revealed that American Express is now able to forecast with eerie accuracy (based on customers' spending habits and where and what they're charging on their credit cards) which of its card members will file for divorce within the next twelve months. You can and should know as much about your customers.

Given how inexpensive technology and analytics have become, it's inexcusable for any business not to know every customer—who's returning, who's new, their purchasing habits, the gross margin and profits they generate, those things they're buying more of, those they're purchasing less of, and if you are meeting or exceeding their expectations. If you lay that kind of analysis over every individual product or service you offer, you'll be able to quickly see what's winning, what's losing, where everything stands, and when it's time to let go.

Ego

The ability of an organization to embrace radical change and reinvention is determined by the ego of the person in charge; substantive change is never initiated from the mid level or bottom ranks of an organization.

Ego*ism* maintains that individuals always do what's in their self-interest, while ego*tism* means having an exaggerated sense of self-importance and narcissism. Both are equally dangerous. Unless the manager, owner, or CEO is able to replace his egotism with healthy ambition, stop doing everything in his own self-interest, and begin doing everything in the interests of the organization, no good change will ever occur.

In health sciences this trap is called the Semmelweis reflex. Austrian physician Ignaz Semmelweis died tragically when he was only forty-seven years old. His autopsy found him a thoroughly broken man physically and mentally, a victim of deep depression and possible beatings, who had died just fourteen days after being committed to an insane asylum outside Budapest.

But what drove him insane is the story behind the Semmelweis Reflex.

Dr. Semmelweis was studying maternity clinics in Vienna in the early 1840s. It was a time before Louis Pasteur and the discovery of invisible germs. Dr. Semmelweis crunched the numbers and found that deadly childbirth fever was highest for new mothers when they delivered their babies in a clinic. In fact, for years many superstitious women suspected this and avoided health care, choosing to have "street births" instead. When Dr. Semmelweis reviewed all of the statistics, he indeed found the street was safer than the clinics. He became a man with a mission.

His gut told him there must be something the doctors were bringing to childbirth that caused the greater mortality rate. He suggested nurses and doctors try careful hand washing in chlorinated lime before each and every examination. Mortality immediately decreased by 85 percent. Semmelweis was thrilled.

But the physicians' egos were bruised. "We're not ignorant tradesmen," they thought, "with filthy hands and necks. Semmelweis has no proof, no science. Washing our hands over and over is a waste of time, time that we should spend attending to our patients. He's crazy."

Semmelweis was ridiculed, ignored, and eventually fired. He wrote letters pleading for more study and made accusations of negligent homicide against those who followed the old ways, but everyone ignored him. It drove the good doctor to a nervous breakdown and ultimately to his tragic time in the asylum. Years later, when Louis Pasteur, John Snow, Robert Koch, Joseph Lister, and others discovered the science he had lacked, Semmelweis was declared a hero, posthumously.

Today we remember him whenever ego reflexively causes someone to reject new knowledge because it contradicts entrenched norms, beliefs, or paradigms.

In extensive research for *Egonomics: What Makes Ego Our Greatest Asset (or Most Expensive Liability)*, authors David Marcum and Steven Smith discovered that 53 percent of businesspeople estimate that ego costs their companies between 6 and 15 percent of their annual revenue, while an additional 21 percent say the total is closer to 20 percent. Even if you use the 6 percent figure, that's still greater than the average profit of each of the Fortune 100 companies.

One need only recall the CEOs of the bankrupt auto manufacturers traveling to Washington, D.C., in their private jets and stretch limos to beg the government for money to understand what happens when a leader's ego causes him to sacrifice results for status, power, and prestige. He is more interested in the world's view of him than in the long-term interests of the company. Ego inevitably leads to arrogance, and arrogance leads to blindness and an inability to recognize good opportunities for growth.

Each time Donald Trump pops up on my television screen uninvited, I find myself imagining what the conversation is like when he meets someone new. I'm willing to bet it starts with the Donald saying, "Now that I've told you about me, why don't *you* tell me about me?"

Keeping one's ego in check requires some serious introspection and answering the most intimate and revealing question anyone will ever ask himself: "Is it all about you, or are you truly doing what you do for the interests and greater good of the organization?"

Unless you can look at yourself in the mirror each morning and with 100 percent certainty know that all the decisions you're about to make and the actions you're about to take are in the long-term interest of the company, you've got (and your company has) a big potential problem.

A good thing to do when you're about to make a decision or embark on a course of action regarding your business is to pause and ask, "Am I doing this for my need to be the center of attention or because it's in the long-term beneficial interests of the company?"

Mel Haught, CEO of Pella Corporation, a company that reinvents five hundred manufacturing processes and operating systems every year, says there are three beliefs common to people with strong egos that they must constantly work to let go of: that they're the smartest people in the room, that the goal is to be perfect, and that they're too busy for dumb questions. Any boss who has to be the smartest person in the room hijacks the dialog, signaling "correct" comments and conclusions that stifle good ideas. Perfectionism opens the door to doing nothing while committees study a strategy to death. Haught says dumb questions force top leaders to reconsider the hidden assumptions that hold back progress (just like they did with those Ford engineers invited to see the new ideas at Toyota).

When the U.S. Army instituted its "uncover your inner jerk" leadership training for new generals, it recommended that the officers ask wives, husbands, sons, and daughters for suggestions for reducing the ego. "They've heard enough and seen enough to know your flaws," candidates were told, "and they are dying to tell you." That's a good idea, and you should do the same, to help you let go and keep your ego in check.

Same Old, Same Old

In *The Leadership Secrets of Colin Powell* (former Chairman of the U.S. Joint Chiefs of Staff and former U.S. Secretary of State) my late good friend, author Oren Harari, put added perspective on the frequently uttered phrase "If it ain't broke, don't fix it," when he added that those words are, in Powell's perspective, "a slogan for the complacent, the arrogant, or the scared."

How can such a commonsense maxim be so insidious and disastrous? It's because of an immutable law of business: *By the time you figure out it's broke, it's been broke for a very long time.* Here's how that happens.

People manage their organizations by the results (revenues and profits), because results are fact based. So if someone is running a simple restaurant, she looks at the end of each day and the end of the month to see how the business is doing. If the evening's gross revenues are within the trend (or better) and the end of the month is profitable, she figures it ain't broke, so she doesn't stress about tinkering with it.

Let's say the food or service is not what customers expect. Some loyal customers will say something like, "You guys are great, but tonight . . . not so much." Most will say nothing. They all will come back, so there's not even a blip on the results radar. Maybe the owner says something to the staff; maybe she doesn't. Maybe the staff changes something and maybe it doesn't. After all, it ain't really broke.

The second time the service or food is disappointing, the loyal customers are still understanding and they underreact again. But the third time it happens the wife looks at the husband with that emasculating "speak up and do something" look, and now they don't come back anymore. But the owner doesn't really notice, because a new customer takes their place, so results are still within the projected range.

Can you see how long it takes? A whole lot of customers, each with their own tolerance level for disappointing service, must be unhappy enough to stop coming, and the total number lost has to be greater than the momentum you've got attracting new customers. If you have more than one profit center or more than one location, or if you run the business from miles away, it just gets harder and harder to react fast enough to derail the suckage freight train.

This happened in the mobile phone business. Sprint was churning (the industry phrase for turning over customers) 40 percent of its customers annually. It banged the marketing drum, creating better data plans and offering free phones to attract new customers. It didn't realize that its dropped calls caused one person after another to say, "That sucks!" and vow to stop using the carrier as soon as their stupid contract was up. When net defections hit 1.2 million customers (new customers minus defecting customers) and losses hit $29.5 billion at one company, headquarters finally got the message. But today, three years later, that poor company is still reeling from the suckage that occurred years before.

"If it ain't broke, don't fix it" is a death knell for any organization hoping to change. The net effect of not challenging or changing anything until it's obviously broken is that a culture is created in which workers and managers become firefighters instead of proactive change agents.

Any business that's constantly sending its managers to fix what's broken will become so preoccupied with temporarily fixing stuff in order to keep things the same that there will never be enough time for proactive reinvention. Businesses that master the art of embracing radical change are quick to fix and change things *before* they're broken, by remembering the words of Andy Grove, who turned Intel into one of the major tech giants on the planet and who said, "Only the paranoid survive."

Notably, an entire school of thought in psychology maintains that managers and leaders who constantly strive to keep things exactly the same, refuse to rock the boat, and do anything to maintain a conflict-free, content environment actually suffer from stilted emotional development brought about by their failure to bond with a primary caregiver when they were infants.

WTGBRFDT—"What's the good business reason for doing this?"—is a question that should be repeatedly asked of everyone by the business owner or manager committed to continuous change. The question should be asked of every product, service, process, and person with the end objective being to make everything better for everyone.

Conventional Wisdom

In recent years, most Western nations have been lucky to grow their economies at a rate of only a couple of percent annually, and most forecasts only promise more of the same. Simple math says that if there were only 2 or 3 percent more to go around each year and everyone were getting their fair share, the achievement of 2 or 3 percent growth would be acceptable.

How many enterprises are you aware of whose big ambition is the achievement of 2 or 3 percent growth? They know (see previous chapter) that modest single-digit growth isn't enough to maintain positive momentum and retain, challenge, and reward great talent.

"Conventional wisdom" is a phrase used to describe ideas or explanations that have been generally accepted as truths based on the past. Using conventional wisdom to predict likely future results in the new century is an innovation killer, because none of the old metrics and rules hold up anymore. One good example is the conventional wisdom surrounding how much money a business should spend on advertising to attract customers.

For years stingy business owners and advertising executives have wagged their fingers at anyone who had a new idea for doing advertising completely differently by dismissing them and pointing out that historically businesses spend between 1 and 2 percent of their annual revenues on advertising and that any amount greater than that is foolhardy. Those numbers have been repeated so many millions of times over the years that people have literally taken them to the bank as vital components of their business plans. Even though Google and Facebook began changing the way businesses advertise, the numbers didn't change, and companies clung to the 2 percent rule that had been handed down through the years.

Then along came young Andrew Mason, with a degree in music (not marketing, advertising, or business) from Northwestern University, who in two short years turned the conventional wisdom about advertising upside down with his startup, Groupon, and who, in the process, built a company poised to go public for upward of twenty billion dollars, and spawned scores of copycat deal sites.

The premise of Groupon is simple. A business that wants to attract new customers comes up with a special offer of 50 percent off the regular price of something really cool that it sells. Groupon e-mails the offer to everyone in its database in the target city or region (it has more than sixty million users worldwide), and as soon as one hundred people have agreed to purchase the offer, the deal is done.

Groupon takes half the money, and the business gets the other half. Conventional wisdom would dictate that the business making the offer made a bad deal and effectively sold something to a hundred people for a 75 percent discount. But Mason saw the folly of all the conventional wisdom surrounding advertising and turned it on its head.

Assume a small bakery that specializes in artisan cupcakes makes an offer on Groupon to sell a dozen of its cupcakes for 50 percent off the regular price of $25.00. When a hundred people agree to buy the deal for $12.50 each, a total of $1,250 is generated, with Groupon taking 50 percent and the retailer the remaining 50 percent. With food costs in most bakeries averaging between 25 and 30 percent it probably cost the business all the money it brought in the door to produce the twelve hundred cupcakes. A dumb business deal? Think again!

Despite the bakery making terrifically good cupcakes, assume that about 30 percent of its first-time customers don't ever return for various reasons. Then assume that another 30 percent become infrequent customers, averaging four visits a year with an average expenditure of twenty-five dollars for each visit, another third become frequent purchasers, averaging ten shopping visits annually and spending twenty-five dollars each time they shop, and the remaining 10 percent become disciples, averaging fifteen or more visits annually and spending twenty-five dollars each time they shop. Those seventy new customers would generate more than $14,250 annually for the small bakery. If the bakery repeated the Groupon offer monthly it would raise its annual revenues by $171,000. That number doesn't take into consideration all the customers who will be referred to the shop by its new customers.

Using conventional wisdom, the bakery owner would have been counseled to spend no more than a few percent of the expected $625 in net cash received for the promotion, which would have given her less than twenty dollars to spend. So much for conventional wisdom!

Companies committed to growth generally target an unconventional minimum of a 5 to 7 percent increase in annual organic growth with a stretch target of 10 percent, but then they proceed to do the dumbest of things and employ conventional wisdom—past truths from an old age—in hopes of achieving their targets. When planning for the achievement of your objectives it's wise to keep in mind the following simple rules:

At its best, conventional wisdom might achieve a conventional result, assuming the wind is at your back and the stars are in alignment.

At its best unconventional wisdom has a chance of achieving an unconventional result.

Any enterprise that dreams of achieving significant growth must be more willing than ever before to embrace new ideas.

If you possess an inquiring mind, then you've already got an advantage on this change killer. But if you don't, the only way to make certain it doesn't become a huge obstacle is to surround yourself with people who are prepared to constantly challenge the status quo.

Good questions to frequently ask are, "Why do we do it this way?" and, "Isn't there a better way to go about doing this?"

Another way to buck conventional wisdom is to surround yourself with energetic young people in your business and then actually listen to them instead of bemoaning that they don't share your same work ethic and they want too much responsibility too soon. The reason young people want responsibility as quickly as possible is because they look around the traditional business landscape and say, "You've got to be kidding me."

Entitlement

Few things stand in the way of radical change and reinvention as much as a sense of entitlement. It's not the sense of entitlement shared by spoiled rich kids. Instead it's the misguided and arrogant belief shared by so many business owners and executives that their business has a right to continue to exist and do well simply by virtue of either being in business or having been successful at some point.

There's no letting go of a sense of entitlement. People who have it are incapable of letting go of anything. They'll spend all their time pointing their fingers at people they think should be doing it for them. People with a sense of entitlement have no place in a leadership position in business. Let go of them.

Greed

When the owners or leaders of a business are self-serving and greedy, treating the company as their own personal pocketbook, there's no chance for any significant change or reinvention to occur. When they talk about change or reinvention it's only in the interest of tweaking things enough to keep things exactly the way they are for as long as possible, in order to fulfill their greed.

Over the past twenty years I've studied a lot of greedy executives. I've watched a few of them let go of their greed only after a tragic event, but it's tough for zebras to change their stripes, and most greedy people remain that way forever; you'd be well advised to steer clear of them.

The conventional wisdom is that greed fuels capitalism. Or at least that it's an inescapable part of the free enterprise personality. Greedy people get extremely defensive, shouting examples and smirking that the other side is hopelessly naive. I've stopped arguing with them.

The very fact that you haven't stopped reading this book is a sign that you're not as trapped by the conventional wisdom about greed as most.

Follow Aristotle's prescription. He said, "We are what we repeatedly do." If you make reinvention a habit, practicing what you learn from this book, you'll let go of greed.

Short-timers

The term *short-timer* refers to someone who is planning on leaving but is still on the job. Predictably, nobody counts on much actual work or productivity from these people, because their heads and interests are elsewhere and they've already emotionally checked out.

During a recent interview with the CEO of a large company in Atlanta, which has a few thousand workers and faces many challenges, the term *short-timer* took on a new dimension as he repeatedly brought up the subject of his summer home in Maine and the big sailboat he keeps there.

By the end of our time together I was convinced his retirement was days or weeks away, because he'd obviously mentally packed his bags and wanted to be in Bar Harbor. As we wrapped up the conversation

I asked how much longer he planned on staying at the helm of the company, and he replied, "Oh, not that long, maybe two or three years. . . . As long as they need me." He concluded with, "I wouldn't want to leave them in the lurch."

This formerly accomplished CEO's comments revealed him to be either extremely selfish or delusional. He may not have wanted to *leave* the company in the lurch, but he was effectively *putting and keeping* the entire organization in the lurch until he finally decided to pull the pin and get his butt out of there. How much radical change or reinvention do you guess he'll initiate during his twilight years at the helm?

CEOs and senior leaders who are thinking about leaving a company have effectively already left, and the biggest favor they can do the organization is to get out of the way and allow the business to change and grow. Well-meaning and well-intentioned leaders who have either self-stamped a sell-by date on their forehead or who have already emotionally checked out are selfishly demanding that the organization put change on the back burner until they decide to throw themselves a good-bye dinner and hand in their keys to the office.

A shared human condition is the desire to leave an organization on an even keel, with everyone sharing fond memories. Those desires are hardly the things that make risk taking, radical change, and reinvention possible.

No organization deserves to have short-timers on the job paying scant attention to detail, possessing bad attitudes, and infecting others with what they have, getting them to fantasize or think about leaving. Short-timers should immediately leave of their own volition or be very quickly shown the door. Unless there are extenuating circumstances, it's good policy that when it's time for those people to move on they do so immediately.

Risk Averse

Being afraid of taking a chance is common.

Coca-Cola had the chance to buy Pepsi for a thousand dollars back when former owner Loft Incorporated went bankrupt, but Coke's representatives told Pepsi's owner they thought the amount being asked made it too risky. Only a decade ago Yahoo had the opportunity to purchase Google for five billion dollars, but then-CEO Terry Semel, following months of negotiation, balked at the price, saying the risk was too great. At the time, the purchase would have represented about 10 percent of Yahoo's value.

For this book I also studied and interviewed a number of companies that haven't embraced change or reinvention and are seemingly risk averse, so I could make some comparisons. One of those companies that hasn't embraced constant change or taken any risks is a large ten-billion-dollar company in the defense space.

Almost all of this company's business units are in the mature part of their life cycle, it's being hard-pressed on margins by many increasingly competent competitors who have recently consolidated, and its leaders readily acknowledge being overly dependent on government contracts in a time when governments have no money. This business is the poster child for a company whose decision makers need to get their heads around change.

While meeting with one of the company's group presidents I asked him why the organization had been so risk averse and reluctant to embrace any change in the recent past. He offered some reasonable explanations and then summed up his response with the following words:

"As an organization we've become so risk averse and unwilling to take a chance on anything that the culture of the organization can best be described as suffering from testicular constrictivitis."

Sadly, his firm has a lot of company suffering from the same ailment.

Dr. Norman Dixon, noted author of *On the Psychology of Military Incompetence*, saw a lot of testicular constrictivitis as he studied commanding officers and their military failures. He found that the most risk-averse commanders were very "anxious under conditions of stress, were prone to be defensive, denied anything that threatened their self-esteem and were bad at judging whether the risks they take or the caution they display are justified by the possible outcomes." Those who had let go of unnecessary anxiety and were more proportional in assessing reality were more likely to be spot-on when they chose to take or forgo action. It's a sad irony, he thought, that the very commanders who are so sensitive to success or failure will be the ones likely to make the biggest mistakes.

Some companies are averse to risk because they've actually seen so many of their peers fail. Famed Harvard professor Clay Christensen, the author of the game-changing *The Innovator's Dilemma*, says that when big companies attempt new things the failure rate is 90 percent. However, the Corporate Strategy Board argues that when venturing into new areas a 99 percent failure rate is more realistic. Most companies are frightened of failure.

American companies' unwillingness to cough up the cash to fund risk taking is even hampering the national economy. For the past forty years companies have invested 100 percent of their cash flow in people, plants, software, capacity, and growth. Today, because of either greed or the uncertainty caused by the near-total financial meltdown of 2008–2009, that number ranges between 50 and 70 percent and most companies have become cash hoarders; it seems that the larger the balance in the bank the bigger they want it to become.

It's irrational to be paralyzed by the fear of risk taking. Half of all new ideas fail because they don't get enough follow-up as they travel from off-site strategy sessions to everyday execution on the front lines. Leaders who troubleshoot their execution process and teach all managers how to get more follow-through can cut the odds of failure in half. There's nothing to fear; just a need to roll up some sleeves.

Then it's a matter of getting a checkup from the neck up. The only guarantee in business is if you do nothing, nothing will happen. Also, as the school of hard knocks teaches, most good strategy is made by doing.

Once you've figured out how you're going to deal with the reinvention killers in your life and business, it will be time to pick a destination and let the radical change begin.

LETTING GO: ACTION PLAN

▶ It's impossible to embrace change and reinvention unless you're able to let go of the reinvention killers: being unable to let go of yesterday's breadwinners; ego; same old, same old; conventional wisdom; a sense of entitlement; greed; a short-timer's mentality; and aversion to risk.

▶ By the time you figure out your business is in trouble, it's been in trouble for a very long time.

▶ Always ask WTGBRFDT (What's the good business reason for doing this?) before making any decision.

▶ Take Colin Powell's advice on the saying "If it ain't broke, don't fix it." He concluded that it's "a slogan for the complacent, the arrogant, or the scared."

▶ If you agree with the research from the best-selling book *Egonomics* (referenced earlier), which reveals that 53 percent of businesspeople believe corporate ego costs their company 6 to 15 percent of their annual revenue, while an additional 21 percent say it costs more than 20 percent, some simple math proves that the true dollar cost of ego to business is greater than the combined net profits (which average slightly less than 4 percent of revenues) of all American companies.

▶ Consider the Semmelweis reflex: rejecting new knowledge because it contradicts your entrenched norms, beliefs, or paradigms.

▶ When the boss has to be the smartest person in the room she'll only receive "correct" comments. When she insists on perfection, time is wasted while stuff is studied to death. Alternately, when "dumb" questions are welcomed, hidden assumptions are challenged.

CHAPTER 3

PICKING THE DESTINATION

The main job of the leader is to be a destination expert, to let everybody know where the company is going and make certain that everyone understands and is willing to embrace constant change in order to get there.

According to legend, the Lakota band of Indians were introduced to what eventually became their nomadic way of life back in the mid-1700s, when they were visited by a holy spirit named Tatanka, who came to them as a buffalo and fulfilled all their needs. The tribes soon came to rely on the buffalo for meat and fat for their food, hides for their dwellings and clothing, and the horns and hoofs for their tools and utensils. Thus began a two-century-long back-and-forth migration by the Lakota from the Great Lakes to the far western United States, following, hunting, and living off the buffalo.

The various Lakota tribes numbered almost forty thousand, and vast numbers of buffalo were required to supply their needs. Further complicating their hard lives following the buffalo was that bows and arrows were the only utensils they had with which to hunt, and they were frequently no match for thundering herds. But somehow the Lakota managed to find and hunt enough of the animals to sustain themselves, until one day it seemed the buffalo were gone for good.

It was as if they'd disappeared.

With great hunger and growing desperation, the hunters of the tribe approached the medicine man for help. "Great and wise one," they pled, "where will we find the next herd of Tatanka? Please point us in the right direction."

The revered medicine man considered their request, took a scrap of buffalo hide, wet it in water, folded it up, and twisted it tightly while imploring the spirits for divine guidance. When his chanting was complete, he smoothed the skin and laid it in the sun to dry.

Slowly, as the hot sun did its work, lines appeared on the skin and the blemishes became reference points. The medicine man lifted the dried skin from the ground and gave the hunters their new "map."

The new trails took the hunters to the right places, and they found fresh game as they had been promised. But the numbers of buffalo weren't as great as before, and the men had to come up with new ways of hunting them.

Instead of shooting their arrows haphazardly at huge herds, they figured out how to force the animals into stone canyons, from which there was no escape. They also figured out how to force a herd of buffalo to stampede off a high cliff, called a "buffalo jump." There are still many jump sites in existence today as historical monuments. Another tactic invented by the hunters was to cover themselves in wolf skins. Because buffalo aren't afraid of wolves, the men could creep close to the herd and then bludgeon them or shoot them with arrows.

All the Lakota hunters needed to become radical reinventors was a clear destination; they figured out the rest of it on their own.

REINVENTION STARTS WITH A CLEAR DESTINATION

We have a history of wanting our leaders to be taller than average. That's probably because in ancient times everyone thought that tall leaders could see farther.

We still want leaders to see far enough to tell us which way to go.

But many CEOs fail. "We aren't sure where the company is headed and can't see how our actions are helping or hurting the cause," almost half of employees, from the front lines to headquarters, said when researchers asked. "We aren't clear about the next steps, either."

It's not that the average CEO shrugs his shoulders when his people ask, "Where are we going?" But his answers are like those from a politician—vague, general, and lacking specifics or clarity. "I need you to plan for different scenarios given all the uncertainty out there," one CEO told his divisional presidents after reviewing the first draft of their operating strategies for the new year. "Also, you need an ambitious strategy to improve productivity," he continued. "Plus, since quality and customer satisfaction are critical to our success, you'd better pay attention to that too." It's not a clear direction; its well-intentioned gobbledygook.

Pat Hassey, who retired in May 2011 as CEO of Allegheny Technologies, is average height but still stands head and shoulders above most other CEOs in the Fortune 1000. He reinvented his company, taking a confused victim of the commoditization of metals manufacturing on the edge of bankruptcy and helping it become one of the nine best performing publicly traded companies from 2001 to 2008. Hassey told me how he made that happen: "My main job is one thing . . . to be the destination expert. I have to be able to see through the fog, see far enough to connect the dots between near and far, and let everybody know where we are going." He then added, "And people don't want to wait forever to find out the destination."

Not having a clear destination means never knowing the steps you need to take to get to where you want to go, never knowing if you've arrived or if you've achieved what you set out to accomplish. But if you have your destination in sight, those things that need to be reinvented will become as obvious as the need to invent new ways of hunting buffalo was for the Lakota Indians.

The destination is partly what the organization does and where it is going, but it also addresses *why* the organization is headed where they are.

REINVENTION TO DIE FOR

The mere mention of death is sufficient to remind most of us of our own mortality, and most business authors would think twice before writing about the funeral business. But there's a story of constant radical reinvention taking place in that industry that's worthy of setting aside our fears about dying to learn some important lessons about picking a destination and the benefit of constant radical reinvention, from a funeral home (of all things) in Saint Petersburg, Florida.

Each year more than 2.5 million people die in the United States Aside from the minute percentage whose bodies are willed to medical science, all the others pass through a funeral home. The business of dying is hugely profitable. More than eleven billion dollars is spent each year with funeral homes, and some estimates argue that if all the peripheral monies, such as flowers, food, music, and car processions, are factored in it's probably closer to fifteen to twenty billion.

More than 80 percent of funeral homes are small family businesses, and for years it was a great business for these mom-and-pop shops. Average six thousand to ten thousand dollars per funeral, do a couple each week with a staff of two or three people, keep your expenses low, and profit margins are more than comfortable. Being a respected and prominent member of the community while making a few hundred thousand dollars a year was very attractive, so these businesses were frequently passed down from father to son with a wink to keep secret just how attractive the business really was.

Unfortunately, one of the absolute laws of free markets is that there's no such thing as a goose that keeps laying golden eggs forever. Just like in Aesop's fable, either the owner of the goose kills it, believing there's a huge lump of gold inside (greed), or someone figures out a way to steal your goose (by doing things better, faster, and cheaper than you).

The forces conspiring to kill the funeral industry's golden goose include the challenges of consolidation, constant negative press about the high cost of dying, and more and more people having little to do with the traditional funerals offered up by organized religion.

But the real game changer confronting the industry is the vast numbers of customers choosing cremation over traditional services. Considering that a customer can buy a cremation for as little as $295, this process threatens to take away more than 95 percent of the typical funeral's yearly revenues.

When the forces of the market are aligned to possibly take away such a large chunk of a company's top line revenues, most businesses react in predictable (and self-destructive) ways. Most funeral home owners simply tried to stop it from happening and took the position of "This isn't going to happen and we're not going to be part of it," and simply refused to offer cremations. Other funeral home owners enlisted their trade and lobbying associations to do everything in their power to prevent anyone who wasn't a licensed embalmer from being in the business; they reasoned that people wouldn't want to enroll in a two-year mortuary sciences program just to get into the business. Others, stuck in another time, reasoned that everyone coming into the business should have to go through the exact same training they'd done decades earlier.

Bill McQueen, owner and CEO of Anderson-McQueen Funeral Home, is an attorney and CPA who took over the family business in 1987, when his father died unexpectedly. "You have to understand," says McQueen, "this is a business that was and is ripe for reinvention. When I took over, everything was done the way it had always been done, because if it was good enough for Dad and Granddad it was supposed to be good enough for me. The real reason things had to change," he says, "was because we had to be able to offer the quality of life that talented people wanted and that we wanted to provide them."

Besides making changes designed to attract and keep the right people, the big challenge facing McQueen was the issue of the already growing number of cremations affecting the company's revenues. "When I took over the business," he says, "cremations had already grown to encompass twenty percent of our business, from only five percent ten years before, and as we entered the 1990s, the dramatic escalation continued and it began having a significant impact on our bottom line, and we decided to seriously get our heads around that part of the business. But we were wrong," he says, "in concluding that everyone wanting a cremation was a price shopper. Originally we thought that by having a low price point for cremations we'd pick up all the price shoppers, plus keep customers who wanted a traditional service."

Anderson-McQueen began advertising low-priced cremations and got a painful surprise. "We discovered that price shoppers *only* want one thing, and that is the absolute lowest price in town, and that they have no regard for value," McQueen says. "And we quickly found ourselves doing more business and our revenues going up a bit but our profits going down even further. We realized that that wasn't a road we wanted to travel."

The breakthrough for McQueen and his brother and sister came from studying cremations in other societies around the world and realizing that in many societies cremation isn't just about dealing with a person's remains but is about ceremony as well. That observation led them to the opening of a cremation tribute center on one of their campuses. McQueen says that first move provided him and the staff with something tangible to get their heads around and talk about.

The success of their first tribute center led McQueen to the realization that they weren't really in the business of handling bodies but were instead in the business of educating and helping people understand the value of ceremony, ritual, and the telling of one's life story. "We weren't going to be in a business that was about caskets, hearses, and cemeteries anymore but instead about helping people transition through loss and come out the other side in a state of peace."

Once they'd selected a destination, the radical reinvention became easy. The first thing to go at Anderson-McQueen was the dark, heavily draped, somber motif. "When you come onto our campuses," says McQueen, "the first thing you'll notice is there are no drapes; just lots of windows and natural light. We want our environments to be uplifting. We got rid of the carpeting and old somber, heavy furniture and replaced it with hardwood floors, Martha Stewart furniture, and baby grand pianos."

The next thing to go was the traditional pricing structure in the industry. According to McQueen, funeral homes traditionally acted as if they didn't charge for their services and instead covered all their costs and profits in the price of a casket. "If someone came in and wanted a top-of-the-line solid mahogany casket that retailed for ten thousand dollars, they paid the same amount whether they wanted three days of visitation and a full church service or a simple ride to the cemetery." McQueen opted for a pricing model that's both à la carte and transparent and that doesn't rely on recovering costs through the sale of merchandise.

The next step in nonstop radical reinvention at Anderson-McQueen was the creation of legacy cafés. "Our cafés look just like a Starbucks," says McQueen, "and we brew complimentary Starbucks coffee and [serve] Otis Spunkmeyer cookies in order to create a familiar environment that's warm, relaxing, and a place where people want to stay and share conversation and family memories."

In rapid succession the company adopted social networking, a presence on Facebook, and the latest video technology, producing slide shows and videos for the grieving families. "We create legacy films that tell a person's life story, have an opening like a great movie, are professionally narrated, and include family members sharing their memories. When you walk into our buildings," says McQueen, "all the lights are on and there are large monitors running videos everywhere, in stark contrast to most funeral homes, where everything is turned off when it isn't being used."

One of the biggest and most radical reinventions occurred in terms of the people the company hired. "When I took over we were totally a male-only organization," says McQueen. "It's almost as though there was an unwritten rule that in order to be a funeral director you had to be a man." Today, the organization's funeral directors are 80 percent female, with most under the age of thirty. "I think that women are naturally better caregivers than men and overall do a better job of nurturing clients," says McQueen, adding, "The joke around our campuses is that the reason it was traditionally an all-male profession is that fifty years ago it was funeral homes that provided ambulance services and men liked to drive the fast cars."

Not all of McQueen's reinventions have met with the approval of those funeral home owners firmly rooted in the dark ages. "I'm sure some people would like to tar and feather me," he says, "but a number of years ago we took the position that loss isn't just about two-legged family members but all family members, and we began offering the same services we offer for people to pet owners. On one of our campuses we created our Rainbow Bridge room, where people can see their pet before it's cremated and hold an event for family members and friends to memorialize their lost family member. We make money offering services for families with pets, but the main thing it allows us to do is reach out, touch people's hearts, and begin building a relationship with them so we can help them with a future loss."

McQueen says he was heavily influenced by the book *The Experience Economy*, by B. Joseph Pine and James H. Gilmore, whose thesis is that we've moved from being an agrarian economy to one based on industry and now to an experience economy, in which our lives are filled with memorable, branded experiences.

"Every business," McQueen says, "needs to turn what they do into a sufficiently memorable experience that people would be willing to pay admission to be part of it. The experience must appeal to all our senses and be participatory. You don't need a mission statement for a business," he asserts, "as much as you need a theme that so resounds with customers that if they were interviewed after leaving your place of business they'd give you a broad smile and a thumbs-up."

McQueen also radically reinvented the customer experience. "Most people in the funeral industry are order takers," he says. "Potential customers make an appointment and show up, are greeted and walked down a dark hall to an office where the vital information is collected, then taken to a depressing room with a bunch of caskets and are asked which one they want to buy and whether or not they want a ceremony."

In order to consistently improve the experience, McQueen says a business owner or leader must ask himself and everyone who works within the organization a very important question every day: "What is the real value that we're providing that allows us to charge the price we ask when people call upon us to serve them?"

McQueen says there was a lot of push-back from staff who didn't agree with the destination and constant reinvention he and his family had in mind for Anderson-McQueen. "Look," he says, "there were a lot of older, long-term employees who didn't like it, and they aren't here anymore. Either they opted out or we opted them out."

How have constant radical change and reinvention affected top line revenues and profits at Anderson-McQueen? According to McQueen, "As recently as seven years ago, when we really embarked on reinvention efforts, we were handling about nine hundred funerals each year. Today, he says, "we're doing more than two thousand and in the process [have] grown our market share from nine percent to more than eighteen percent."

Invariably, when highly talented and determined people who are committed to growing their businesses witness the positive effects of reinvention, they become addicted and become serial reinventors; Bill McQueen is no exception. "We're committed to change and growth," he says. "That might take the form of acquisitions, regional growth, or horizontal expansion by moving into other life event areas like weddings and anniversaries." He is careful to point out that all moves depend on having the right people in place.

When Bill McQueen was asked if he was reluctant to share the story of his business and commitment to constant reinvention, he replied, "Not at all. Lots of people come and visit us to see and learn what we're doing, but they're all either reluctant to put up the money to make change happen, become worried that it's too hard to do, or don't know how to begin. As for us," he continues, "we're so busy trying to constantly change and grow our business that I don't give much thought to them."

The proper selection of a destination is vital. A business owner or manager can rely on the following to help him or her select a destination for the enterprise:

Data and analytics

Careful listening to customers

Big, bright ideas that are far ahead of what the customer thinks he or she needs or wants

Data and Analytics

Kmart tore up the retail world in the 1970s, opening hundreds of superstores every year. By the end of the decade it had replaced Sears as America's top retailer and began acquiring others to fuel more growth—PayLess Drug, Sports Authority, and OfficeMax, as well as pizza-video parlors and other restaurant chains.

Meanwhile, in a small town way off the beaten path, a pint-size competitor took a different path. This company used every spare penny to buy point-of-sale data systems and satellite links to make reorders automatic and wring all excess inventory costs out of the supply pipeline. By the end of the 1980s it had built a significant inventory-management and logistics advantage over every other company in retail; its computing power was second only to that of the U.S. government.

Quickly, the mighty Kmart found itself far behind this analytically savvy upstart from Bentonville, Arkansas, in saving customers money. By 1990, Walmart had replaced Kmart as the number one retailer. Unable to catch up, Kmart shuttered 110 stores in 1994, and by 2002 the company had filed for Chapter 11 bankruptcy.

Hundreds of smart, fast competitors have followed Walmart, using data and analytics to see farther and save money.

One of the best examples is Capital One.

Rich Fairbanks still can barely believe what he's done. The son of a Stanford University physics professor and himself a top scholar, Fairbanks grew up with a love for empirical data. His second love was business. He was determined to marry the two by starting a business. "But how do you start a company," he wondered, "when you have no experience, no money, and no business ideas?"

In 1987 Fairbanks landed a gig studying the credit card business of a New York bank. On day one he had his "a-ha" moment. The credit card industry could be the ultimate scientific laboratory, he realized, "where every decision about product design, channels of communication, customer selection, pricing, collection policies, everything could be subjected to systematic testing." Data, facts, and proof would lead the way to terrific and profitable business decisions.

Fairbanks shopped his data-driven concept to twenty of the top twenty-five credit companies. But the banks scoffed at his thesis. They had a tight grip on their decades-old ideas and practices, much like that monkey from the previous chapter.

However, the little Signet Bank, in Richmond, Virginia, wasn't trapped by the big banks' conventional wisdom. Its leaders said that Fairbanks (and his consulting partner, Nigel Morris) could crunch numbers, observe operations, track results, test alternate ideas, and use the data to fix their fledging credit card business.

It was a brilliant strategy. By 1994 Fairbanks and Morris's operation alone was worth $1.1 billion and is now the fifth-largest provider of credit cards in America. Fairbanks continues to let data pick the next destination for Capital One.

Careful Listening to Customers

Companies spend almost twenty billion dollars worldwide asking questions and compiling answers from their customers. With all that research you'd expect they'd have a good idea what customers are thinking. Yet most executives don't have any idea. Consider:

- About 250,000 new products are launched each year and expected to sizzle. Yet 85 to 95 percent fizzle!

- When the Product Development Institute studied innovative sizzlers and fizzlers, the fizzlers all were totally confident they understood customer needs, despite their terrible batting average.

- Most executives don't even know whether they are a disappointment to their best customers. When asked, "Do you provide a superior experience for your customers?" four out of five executives replied, "You bet we do!" But nine out of ten of their customers were surprised when they heard that answer. "They told you our experience was superior?" customers asked with a sigh. "Well, it's not!"

Research can't tell you everything you need to know.
Twenty-five years ago high-tech companies did a lot of consumer testing, asking people, "What do you want?" Apple's Steve Jobs didn't believe in that. "How can I possibly ask somebody what a graphics-based computer [one that uses a graphic user interface, or GUI, like the first Mac and Windows products] ought to be?" he asked CEO John Sculley. "No one has ever seen one before!"

Listening starts with leaders getting their hands dirty.

SAS Institute, based in Cary, North Carolina, is the most highly regarded business analytics company in the world. Its products and services are used at more than fifty thousand sites in over 127 countries, including 93 of the top 100 companies on the 2011 Fortune Global 500® list, and it is consistently voted the best company to work for in the United States. What's ironic is that the best analytics company largely employs an old-fashioned methodology for much of its own research. "Our destination," says company founder and CEO Dr. Jim Goodnight, "is to be the single most valued weapon in business decision making." Toward that end, Goodnight spends much of his time doing what he learned in his freshman computer course: talking with and listening to customers and finding out their needs. In his inimitable low-key but rapier sharp manner Goodnight asks a most important question: "How in the world can any company create something of value if they don't first find out what their customers are trying to achieve?"

SAS goes as far as involving its customers in each new service or product it creates. Goodnight explains that in SAS's move from being a tools provider to a solutions provider it made sense to involve client partners at every step of the creation/invention process, to ensure that the new product addresses real problems specific to an industry.

Additionally, SAS compiles an annual SASware Ballot, based on all the comments and suggestions that come into its tech support unit; these become the basis for suggestions to enhance its global suite of products. The company then sends the ballot out to all its customers to vote on their top preferences.

At Honda Motor Co. they call getting your hands dirty *sangen shugi* ("experience it"). Executives are expected to connect with customers and see the actual product, in the actual place, being used by the actual customer. Once, in the parking lot at Disneyland, Honda's designers saw people struggling to get strollers and other awkward items in and out of car trunks. They immediately redesigned the trunks on upcoming models. Innovations like that catapulted Honda to the top tier of imported car manufacturers.

Worldwide fashion retailer H&M aims to accomplish the same with executives working in the stores and visiting the streets, clubs, and events to connect with customers.

Now that Howard Schultz is back at Starbucks he's reconnecting his headquarters with his customers. "We want to put our feet in the shoes of the customers," he says. "We have people in Seattle who want a blueberry muffin in the stores and people in China who say, 'I think black sesame is probably what the customers would rather have.' Well, we're going to appeal with great respect to local tastes and not show the hubris of the past. It's time to trust the people in the marketplace to better know their markets than the people in Seattle."

Big, Bright Ideas That Are Far Ahead of What the Customer Thinks He or She Needs or Wants

How do you land on a bright idea that's ahead of what your customer thinks he or she needs or wants? One way is to follow the lead of Ted Taylor.

Ted Taylor was the son-in-law of pioneer Salinas, California, produce grower and reinventor Bruce Church. In 1926 Church became famous for using ice to keep his lettuce crisp as it traveled by rail from California to Maine, creating a national business for himself. (He's the guy responsible for "iceberg" lettuce.) Ted followed in his father-in-law's footsteps by using a recipe of nitrogen, oxygen, and carbon dioxide in chilled railcars to extend freshness even longer.

But Taylor's deepest desire was to get his family business out of the commodity marketplace altogether. In those days growers squeezed a paltry one or two cents' profit out of every head of lettuce. Taylor invented a way to sell that same head of lettuce for five times more, making considerably more money.

He washed it, chopped it, mixed in some shredded carrots or other kinds of greens, and put it all in a high-tech twelve-ounce bag that would keep everything delicious for weeks instead of days. Families got healthy salad, ready to eat; stores got a more profitable, more popular item while cutting down on spoiled produce; and Taylor reinvented his company as a six-hundred-million-dollar player, in the process creating a brand-new business category, selling salad instead of just lettuce.

What Taylor did was first written about as a best practice back at the turn of the twentieth century. It was called the Law of the Situation. A window shade manufacturer was advised by the first female business consultant, "Don't look at your business as being a maker and installer of wooden blinds. See yourself through your client's eyes. You are actually in the lighting control business."

Once you've selected a destination, it's time to begin making lots of small bets to get you there.

PICKING THE DESTINATION: ACTION PLAN

▶ Figure out what business you are really in or want to be in. Always be on the lookout for a way to turn lettuce into salad.

▶ Constantly communicate the destination of the business to *everyone*, in a way that is clear, concise, and easily understood.

▶ Make certain everyone can recite the businesses destination in one sentence or less. Ask ten different people a day to recite it for you.

▶ The right people have internal GPS systems that will help them figure out what needs to be radically changed if the destination is clear to them.

▶ Constantly urge everyone in the organization to be on the lookout for potential game changers, embrace them early, and reward them for doing so.

▶ What was good enough for Granddad and Dad is irrelevant.

▶ If you're building a business model based *only* on low price, remember that price shoppers only want the cheapest price.

▶ Turn the purchase of whatever you make, sell, produce, or do into a branded and themed experience, constantly tweaking each component of the experience in order to improve it.

▶ Practice the Taoist definition of leadership: Find a parade and walk in front.

▶ Change the physical environment from old, privileged, and stuffy to new, exciting, and collaborative. Get rid of private offices and the hushed, closed-door conversations they encourage, in favor of cubicles. Dump old furniture in favor of new and sleek. Make walls of golf trophies and pictures taken with politicians against the rules for everyone. The environment should shout, "We're here to create and change the world."

▶ Give everyone a seat at the table. Unless your company is filled with people who look like your customers and are your customers, you'll never radically reinvent anything.

▶ Data and analytics: Know everything there is to know about your customers and their past shopping or purchasing habits, employ technology to forecast likely future purchases, and constantly experiment with steps that can be taken to build their loyalty and increase their intent to repurchase.

▶ Keep everyone's hands dirty: Develop an institutionalized program of listening to your customers and potential customers. All workers should be taught the skills needed to be more interested than interesting. Employees at every level should be engaged in the listening process.

▶ Encourage and reward big, bright ideas that are far ahead of what the customer thinks he or she needs or wants. The reward should be proportionate to the economic value the idea generates.

▶ Create some chaos. When Anderson-McQueen started offering funeral and memorial services for pets, most other funeral directors became so apoplectic they almost needed the firm's services. Good!

▶ Get those workers who don't agree with the company's destination to opt out, or opt them out.

CHAPTER 4

KISS A LOT
OF FROGS

"The successful don't start with brilliant ideas . . . they discover them!"

—Peter Sims, best-selling author
and venture capitalist

"Go big or go home," Chris White, the new managing director of the Nestlé Kit Kat brand in the UK, reasoned.

Nestlé's worldwide CEO had noticed White's earlier performance in Australia, where he'd significantly improved ice cream sales, and sent him to England to fix the ailing Kit Kat chocolate bar brand, which had not only seen sales fall by 10 percent the previous year but had also lost its prestigious position as Britain's number one snack after more than seventy years.

The stakes for the new man in charge were huge. The average British consumer eats more than twenty pounds of chocolate confections each year. Collectively, it's a twelve-billion-dollar market, and Nestlé doesn't like to lose.

The forty-one-year-old new executive felt a rush and leapt into action. "We'll scrap the old marketing and advertising slogan [which he proclaimed in media interviews to be in "crisis"] and just roll out loads of new flavors, and it will be déjà vu—just like the job I did in Australia—all over again."

And so the slogan "Have a break, have a Kit Kat," which every British citizen between the ages of the cradle and the grave could instantly recite, was scrapped. Under the direction of the new boss, a dizzying array of new flavors flooded the market. Within just a year, Blood Orange, Christmas Pudding, Dark Chocolate, Lemon and Yogurt, Lime Crush, Mango and Passion Fruit, Red Berry, Seville Orange, Strawberries and Cream, and White Chocolate were all brought to market.

It looked like White's audacious big bet might work. During the first twelve months the four-year sales decline was reversed, but then things quickly took a turn for the worse and the chocolate really hit the fan.

First, ominous rumblings were heard. Retailers reported complaints from customers. "It tastes strange," one said. "Sickly sweet," said another, making a face like he had accidentally swallowed a bug.

"We're getting some blowback," the sales managers acknowledged. The new flavors began clogging the warehouses' aisles. "Do you know why we call you a sales *force*?" the managing director responded when his managers brought him the feedback. "Because sometimes you have to use a little *force* to get things done!"

They put the hammer down and continued to flood the market.

Discount deals were made, some cutting the price by 95 percent (twenty-dollar packages of the new candy bars were sold for just ninety cents). Salespeople were added, and new accounts were opened, with promises to use the new displays and place the product prominently. But even at huge discounts, the numbers of disappointed customers continued to grow, until there was a resounding chorus of, "I've always loved a Kit Kat, but this stuff is absolutely rubbish."

This brash big bet cost Nestlé dearly. Not only did the huge line extension flop and embolden competitors such as Mars to badmouth Kit Kat and make inroads with customers, but sales of the Kit Kat brand, a longtime favorite of British candy lovers, declined another 16.8 percent. The entire company took a huge hit.

"They've ripped up a hundred years of brand investment," said an industry insider, explaining how disappointment had turned into a double-digit decline.

The self-assured Mr. White had made a single big bet and kissed one frog expecting it to turn into a prince, but had forgotten the rule of frogs and princes.

You need to kiss a lot of frogs to find a prince!

Mr. White was no longer in charge.

THE FAIRY TALE OF THE BIG BET

People are 120 times more likely to die by being hit by lightning and twelve hundred times more likely to die from a bee sting or snakebite than to win the lottery, but they still line up to buy lottery tickets. While it's one thing to occasionally wager a dollar on nearly impossible odds, it would be insane to sell your house and cash in your life savings to place a single bet on impossible odds, but that's what many people in business routinely do. Why?

Each day thousands of small and midsize companies make big, one-shot bets—and fail. We don't hear about most of them, just as we don't hear about people who lose the lottery; they aren't front-page news. News isn't interested in these "dog bites man" or common, everyday stories, because they don't drive ratings or page views. Instead, the press gives us "man bites dog" stories of big bets and immodest success. The constant repetition reinforces the myth of business as a high-stakes lottery in which the winners go big or go home.

Peter Sims, best-selling author and venture capitalist, saw the big-bet fairy tale firsthand while attending Stanford Graduate School of Business. "We'll do something new, start a company or take an unconventional career path," his fellow MBA students would say to him, "but we need a great [big] idea first." In other words, they believed billion-dollar ideas were the starting point for entrepreneurs. "But Google started as a small library search project; Starbucks had no chairs and nonstop opera music at the beginning," Sims says. "Great entrepreneurs didn't start with big ideas, for the most part." When business owners, MBAs, and senior executives buy into this fairy tale they often end up with unhappy endings, dashed dreams, careers in ruins, fortunes lost, and unemployed workers.

Recall the big-bet merger that Carly Fiorina engineered with Compaq after she became CEO of HP. It was a disaster that resulted in the company's stock falling by more than half during her tenure.

Likewise, Stanley O'Neal's big bet on reckless investments brought Merrill Lynch to its knees and forced the company into the hands of Bank of America.

The big bet that Time Warner's former CEO Gerald Levin engineered with AOL will go down as the worst deal in business history and cost shareholders more than two hundred billion dollars.

Bob Allen, former CEO of AT&T, nearly destroyed the company when he made a single big bet and acquired computer company NCR. The bet turned out to be so bad that the combined company lost twelve billion dollars, the normally staid *Time* magazine called it a "monolithic screw-up," and the only way the company was saved was by laying off fifty thousand employees.

Then there's Angelo Mozilo, the former CEO who became so blinded by success that he bet his entire company, Countrywide Home Loans, on subprime mortgages and who will forever be the poster child for the housing and mortgage meltdown that almost destroyed the American economy.

Businesses that do the best job of constant radical change and reinvention simply don't get blinded by the fairy tales of the biggest bets generating the biggest paydays. They realize that successful strategy is discovered by doing, and that doing has to be learned from making lots of small bets.

MAKE LOTS OF SMALL BETS

"My parents bet everything when my dad left his job and founded the company, and we were forced to bet everything again when we had to leave the milk solids distribution business for our current model," says John Tracy, CEO of family-owned Dot Foods. "But we've worked too hard, too long, and are responsible for the lives and well-being of too many people [thirty-five hundred at last count] to risk it all. Instead," says Tracy, "we make lots of carefully thought-out small bets."

When I first wrote about Dot Foods in my book *Think Big, Act Small* in 2005, the company had distinguished itself as one of only ten U.S. companies that had achieved double-digit organic revenue and profit growth for ten consecutive years, between 1995 and 2005.

The business model of Dot Foods is deceptively simple. The company purchases huge amounts of food from manufacturers, warehouses those purchases, and then provides a weekly delivery to its distributor clients—in essence distributing to distributors. The brilliant business model relieves individual food-service distributors from having to tie up huge amounts of money in inventory they might not need or being forced to order the huge minimums required by manufacturers. It also alleviates the need for manufacturers to maintain sales relationships with each of the nation's more than ten thousand food-service distributors.

The company makes money three ways: It purchases full truckloads from manufacturers and sells those products to distributors at a slightly higher price; manufacturers pay the organization for transporting their goods; and it receives a sales and distribution allowance from the manufacturers for relieving or assisting them with those functions.

One of the many things that impressed me about this family-owned company in Mount Sterling, Illinois, was their commitment to nonstop change and innovation. I became curious as to how they'd weathered the Great Recession and the role that constant change and reinvention had played in their business success.

It turns out that the company's enviable track record of double-digit annual revenue growth has continued in each of the years since 2005; the company has doubled in size to nearly four billion dollars in annual revenues. Not a bad performance for a family-owned business founded in the living room by Robert Tracy; funded with a mortgage on their twenty-thousand-dollar home; and whose original employees were Robert, who did the selling, and his wife, Dot, who did the bookkeeping, order entry, and delivery coordination, all while raising twelve children. One early shared family memory is of Dot loading as many of the children who could fit into the family station wagon, filling it with bags of milk solids, and making daylong delivery trips across Illinois.

A few years ago, Pat Tracy, the company's chairman, passed the CEO's torch to his brother John.

"Our destination is to be the best in class at delivering supply chain solutions to the food industry," says Tracy. "In order to accomplish that we need to stay ahead of our customers' needs. Every customer, supplier, broker, and group that we work with is constantly seeking solutions, new products, and new ways of doing things, and it's our job to be constantly innovating and making lots of small bets to make sure we stay ahead of their needs."

Bucking conventional wisdom, Tracy says, "When the recession hit we immediately started investing even more money in more new initiatives. We promoted a bunch of people who we thought had a lot of potential and gave them each some money and some people and started immediately chasing new opportunities and making some small bets we thought could become big parts of our business down the road.

"We sell to distributors, and many sell to chain restaurants, but we'd never spent much time with them, so we began a national accounts initiative to work in conjunction with our distributor customers and began working directly with them on their supply chain issues, trying to make everything more efficient for everyone," says Tracy. "Another brand new area," he says, "is the retail side of the health and beauty business, which has us working with supermarkets and convenience stores for the first time."

"We found another need in the cheese business," says Tracy. "We've always worked with Land O'Lakes and Kraft, but our distributor customers always had a problem finding and stocking high-quality import and domestic specialty cheeses for their gourmet, high-end, white-tablecloth customers, so we made a bet in that area as well." The company also moved quickly into protein—specifically beef and pork—which quickly became a huge part of Dot Foods' growth in the past two years.

When asked what keeps him awake at night in his new role, John responds, "Innovation and constant change got us to where we are and are still what drives the business." He adds, "Our big challenge is making certain that every one of our workers understands that every little piece of innovation or reinvention that they can bring to the table—whether they're a truck driver, a warehouse person, or a senior executive—is going to add to our ability to compete and grow long-term.

"I've never seen any company that stopped doing what made them successful not get a severe case of the hiccups. We don't need and we don't want the hiccups," he says, "and the best way to avoid them is to keep the values that have served us so well, never stop embracing constant change and innovation, and continuing to share the growth with everyone." He concludes, "*Everyone* is defined as the workers, customers, and communities."

STARBUCKS TAKES SMALL STEPS TO GET BIG REWARDS

When Howard Schultz stepped down as CEO of Starbucks in 2000, the company had enjoyed one of the most incredible runs of any global brand, having grown to more than sixteen thousand stores in fifty countries. Even though Schultz remained the company's chairman, there's general agreement that in the years that followed, the company's rapid expansion caused it to lose much of its brand's luster and soul. Then, the recession hit. Customer traffic dropped precipitously, there was widespread employee dissatisfaction, and many analysts who followed the company doubted the course could be corrected.

When Schultz retook the CEO reins in 2008 the first thing he did, he told the *Harvard Business Review*, "was admit to ourselves and the people within the company that we owned the mistakes we'd made." Schultz credits that admission as the first big turning point toward Starbucks' turnaround.

Next, in an effort to regain a sense of teamwork and reestablish the values within the organization, Schultz took ten thousand Starbucks workers to New Orleans for a leadership conference, where they spent hundreds of thousands of hours volunteering to rebuild the Katrina-ravaged city.

Additionally, in an effort to stop the bleeding, in one fell swoop Schultz closed one thousand underperforming stores, eliminated seven thousand positions, revised the business plan downward to numbers they could hit, and embraced radical change and began making a dizzying series of small bets. Here are a few of the small bets placed by the company within the first eighteen months of Schultz's return:

▶ **New store design**—In record-breaking time Starbucks developed four new store designs. Each new or renovated store is now either a *Heritage* coffeehouse, reflective of the mercantile roots of the company's first Seattle store; an *Artisan* store, echoing the industrial past of urban markets; a trendsetting *Regional Modern* store; or a *Concept* store, which the company refers to as its design sandbox.

▶ **Wine and beer**—In 2010 the company opened one of its learning-lab stores and began selling beer and wine. If the bet pays off, the company will roll out this model wherever possible.

▶ **New products**—Since Schultz's return the company has been furiously churning out new products, ranging from Cocoa Cappuccino to Starbucks Petites, which includes Cake Pops, Whoopie Pies, and Mini Cupcakes.

▶ **Mobile payments**—In 2011 Starbucks debuted a mobile phone app at all U.S. stores that allows customers to simply hold their phone in front of a scanner to pay for their purchase.

▶ **Big push in digital media**—Schultz believes there's a seismic shift in consumer behavior and has made bets on Facebook, Twitter, and Foursquare; it's already paying off by dropping the cost of customer acquisition.

▶ **Free Wi-Fi**—In 2010 Starbucks made free and unlimited Wi-Fi available at all of its stores, including free access to sites with a paywall, such as wsj.com.

▶ **Via Ready Brew instant coffee**—The instant coffee market is worth more than twenty billion dollars. Starbucks entered the fray with Via and quickly made it available in Costco, Target, and thirty-seven thousand other retail locations. Via achieved sales of more than one hundred million dollars during the first twelve months on the market.

▶ **New logo**—For forty years the Starbucks logo featured a siren (a woman whose enchanting singing lured unwary sailors onto the rocks) inside a circle surrounded by the words *Starbucks Coffee*. In 2011 the logo was changed: The words disappeared and the siren stands alone. Schultz says this allows the company to start thinking of itself as far more than just a coffee seller.

▶ **Starbucks Rewards card**—When you sign up for the new Starbucks reward card you get a free beverage on your birthday, a star for every purchase, and free drinks and dollar-off offers as you accumulate points. Earn thirty stars and you become a gold member, with even more goodies.

▶ **Starbucks Perfect Oatmeal**—This is an example of a small bet becoming a home run. Introduced at the end of the recession, it was proclaimed the company's most successful launch ever. Starbucks hasn't disclosed the revenues generated by oatmeal, but some analysts have guessed it's as much as five hundred million dollars in annual sales (if each Starbucks location sold thirty servings of oatmeal a day that number would easily be achieved.)

▶ **Tea**—With worldwide tea sales growing as much as 20 percent annually, Starbucks has made a bet on tea and offers scores of specialty tea drinks.

▶ **Doubling the number of stores in China**—Starbucks is coming close to having as many stores outside the U.S. as it does stateside, and it's placed one of its bets on China, where it's adding several hundred stores annually.

▶ **Real-time monitors**—Further demonstrating its commitment to social media, Starbucks has strategically placed large flat screens throughout its corporate headquarters so that everyone can not only see but is forced to see what the world is saying and posting about the company on Facebook and Twitter.

It's significant that the revenue generated by the large numbers of small bets Howard Schultz made after retaking control of Starbucks is almost equal to the company's total annual profit. In a good year Starbucks earns about one billion dollars on revenues of ten billion;

the incremental revenue generated by his many small bets exceeds the company's total average annual profits. A strong argument can be made that without the many small bets he made—excluding their potential effect on future revenues and profits—the company would still be struggling to make a profit.

HOW MANY SMALL BETS SHOULD YOU MAKE?

Every enterprise should be continually making as many small bets as can adequately be handled without disrupting the core business or putting it at risk. A small business with a handful of employees might be able to handle two or three concurrent small bets, while a large company with thousands of employees should probably be considering hundreds of potential small bets and implementing scores of them. Consider the following criteria when making your small bets:

▶ Don't plan on only hitting home runs. In baseball, the odds of hitting a single are 1 in 6; a double, 1 in 21; while the odds of hitting a homer are 1 in 35. Unless your name is Babe Ruth or Willie Mays, you probably shouldn't plan on hitting them all out of the park.

▶ Make as many small bets as you have people responsible for making them happen and sufficient financial resources to maximize the odds of success. If there aren't enough resources to give the small bet a chance, you'll never know if it might have worked out or been a possible home run.

▶ Make as many small bets as you're able with enough time available to analyze and learn from each. Most people make a small bet and then start penciling themselves into oblivion by performing Chinese math as they reason, "Hmm, there are 1.4 billion people in China and if only one percent buy what we sell that's 140 million sales and we're going to be stinking rich overnight." When someone embraces Chinese math, greed and impatience almost always take over and the small bet quickly becomes a risk-everything proposition. Baseball players don't get second chances at the plate—three strikes and they're out. Businesspeople are given a second or third chance to turn singles and doubles into eventual home runs, if they take the time to learn from each experience.

▶ Have some general backup ideas in mind, but don't let the backup plan be carved in stone. That will prevent you from learning. The time to begin building formalized backup plans is during the tweaking, changing, and maneuvering that occurs while studying the results of the small bet. Backup plans become vital when a small bet that's turned out to be successful is about to be scaled in size.

Make enough small bets that everyone knows they're being made and that doing so becomes a vital part of the culture of the organization. I have a friend, Mike McCallister, who is the CEO of Humana, a large health insurance company in the U.S. He began a long and illustrious career as a CEO of hospitals while still in his early twenties, and each time he took over another hospital he would direct the maintenance department to begin painting something. "Seeing painters at work and smelling fresh paint," he says, "sent a signal to everyone that change was happening." Making lots of small bets sends a signal that something is always happening and that there's always a good reason to show up for work.

CREATING A CULTURE OF SMALL BETS

A culture of small bets is a learning culture in which people discover the right paths to new destinations. In these organizations work is often less like executing a blueprint and more like crossing a fast-moving stream by jumping from rock to rock. Decisions are made in the moment, without perfect information, and people experiment by changing variables, staying in motion, and conquering their fears, with the ultimate destination always clear in their mind's eye.

"This takes skills we don't learn in school, even business school," author Peter Sims explains. "In school, we are conditioned to play by a very conventional set of rules." What we need is a new set of rules.

Learn in Loops

Sims thinks business could learn a lot from comedian Chris Rock. "When he performs on HBO he's considered brilliantly creative and innovative. Yet his approach is the result of lots of little bets, where he goes into clubs in front of thirty or forty people with some crude starting points and then improvises off his list of ideas, most of which fail [or "bomb," as Rock calls it]."

Looping through that process day in and day out, he's able to identify where the surprises and the big laughs are going to be for the HBO audience. It's an iterative approach that discovers the best material, meaning he adjusts his small bets—changing words, tone, timing, or some other specific element of the joke—and tells it again to see what will give him the desired result. He does all this in real time under real conditions (in Rock's case that's onstage in a stand-up club). This cycle repeats until he has an outstanding ninety minutes.

Rock is so successful because, according to Sims, "Chris has the right mind-set for it—he's resilient, persistent, not afraid of being imperfect or even bombing."

Make Small Bets Smart Bets

Many executives hurry to make bets based on gut feelings or what seems to be common sense among peers. "We need to introduce our new software to market and generate some leads," a sales VP will tell her marketing manager. "Let's do two hundred thousand dollars' worth of direct mail. And we need this in their hands yesterday, so get going."

From this experiment executives will decide all kinds of things. Does direct mail still work? Is the new marketing team creative enough? Can that marketing manager manage? Does the product have good potential? Of course, none of the answers will be reliable, because the bet started with a vague destination and people jumped to all their conclusions. It's not very smart.

SMART is an acronym you need to remember every time you make a small bet. It stands for specific, measurable, accountable, resourced, and timed.

Specific: There is a detailed destination. In the previous example, SMART starts with specifically how many customers they wanted to find and how that justifies spending two hundred thousand dollars.

Measurable: Create a detailed road map with markers from the destination back to the starting point—in this case from the number

91

of customers sold back to the number of prospects needing to be contacted.

Accountable: Decide who is responsible at every checkpoint in the road map.

Resourced: Answer the tough questions. Is there enough time, money, and experience budgeted? It's important to realize that the three are interdependent, so the lack of any one means you'll need more of the other two.

Timed: Adhere to deadlines every step of the way so that someone can track the follow-through and know that what's expected is getting done.

Give Teams Good Feedback

Your people need feedback. But a lot of the feedback managers give isn't very good. Think about this simple demonstration.

Twelve people are evenly divided into three teams. Each team has one teammate blindfolded, who is given a ball to toss into a trash can placed ten feet away. Each team gets ten attempts; the challenge is to make the most baskets.

The first group (representing the end-of-the-year performance review school of feedback) doesn't say anything until the blindfolded teammate has completed all ten attempts. Then they give the shooter feedback such as, "Your first shot was long and left, the next fell short . . ." and so on.

The second group (representing the always positive but maddeningly vague I'm-okay-you're-okay school of feedback) speaks to the shooter freely, but they restrict their comments to generic phrases like "Good job" or "Keep trying; we believe in you," with lots of encouraging words but never anything specific.

The third group works without restrictions. They give their shooter immediate detailed instructions about how and where the last lob missed and offer advice about force, trajectory, and direction. They even take some time for questions.

At the end of the complete first round, which team is most likely to have the best results? How about at the end of a second round? Most important, which blindfolded team member will be the most enthusiastic about being handed the ball for a second or third round?

Your answers tell you all you need to know about creating a framework for good feedback—make it timely, relevant, and helpful.

No Skunking

The CEO at Dot Foods said this one question kept him from having a good night's sleep: "How do we make sure that each member of our team knows that every piece of innovation or reinvention counts no matter how small it is? Everyone has to contribute regardless of their position in the company if we are going to remain competitive in the marketplace and expand in the long-term."

It's a worry on the minds of many CEOs.

The fact is most people come to work with a spark of creativity and a desire to help the cause. But along the way, that spark gets extinguished. The solution is to adopt a "no skunking" principle among mangers and senior personnel.

Skunking is defined as spraying negativity on the creative spark in a coworker or subordinate. It can be an impatient look that says, "That's a dumb question," or a conversation-killing shot like, "We tried that and it didn't work."

Gordon MacKenzie, the late author and creative genius behind Hallmark for many years, illustrated the terrible effects of skunking on creativity. He saw it firsthand in his many visits to elementary schools.

"I'm an artist," MacKenzie would say, introducing himself to the kindergarten class. "Are any of you artists like me?" All the hands in the room would go up, with half of the room waving both hands. "They weren't just creative. They were enthusiastic."

He got similar results when he asked the same question in the first grade. A little less enthusiasm maybe, only one hand in the air instead of two waving hands, but everybody still considered themselves to be creative.

Second grade showed some noticeable fallout. Many in the room raised their hands, but a significant few concluded, "No, I'm not an artist. I'm not that creative." They kept their hands in their laps.

As MacKenzie continued to the third, fourth, and fifth grades the percent of the class who identified themselves as creative, believing they were artists like MacKenzie, continued to fall. Finally, when he asked sixth graders, "Who is an artist like me?" only two hands would go up. And they both would put up their hands nervously, checking to make sure nobody was laughing or saying derisively, "Look who thinks she's creative."

What do you think happened to all the artists? The kindergarten was full of creative types. Did their families move? Did they all transfer to an art school?

You know the answer. Year after year, project after project, somebody sprayed the kids with negativity, telling them what was wrong with their efforts. And all that negativity chipped away at their good opinions of themselves. By sixth grade almost everyone had gotten the message: "Better not put your hand up. You'll just get shot down."

The same thing will continue to happen in your business, unless you implement a no-skunking principle. As MacKenzie says, "Nothing will extinguish the flames of innovation more rapidly than a punitive response to ideas or actions."

It's Okay to Make Mistakes

It was an unexpected conclusion that rocked the Harvard research team. "Well-led teams have higher error rates than average or poorly led teams," the researchers concluded. Harvard was studying acute-care hospitals and other settings, including executive boardrooms. The results were consistent: Teams led by the best leaders made significantly *more* mistakes.

This data proved the opposite of what Professor Amy Edmondson had predicted. But when she dug deeper to uncover why good leaders get such bad results, she found a root cause that was even harder for everyone to swallow.

In fact, what they thought was that the "average error rate" in mission-critical settings was wrong. Poorly led teams "systematically underreported" their mistakes. In layman's terms, they covered up their mistakes.

The CEO of a large Midwestern healthcare group wanted to reinvent her acute-care hospitals. She determined that to reduce medical errors she had to stop teams from covering up any errors. "We've got to believe it's okay to make mistakes."

Her thinking was simple and yet so sophisticated. The complex health-care environment has numerous near misses every day, in which someone notices a mistake or misunderstanding, realizes the error will lead to a poor outcome, and steps in to fix the situation before it becomes a statistic. However, this CEO reasoned that if people also reported the details of every near miss, they could create systems or procedural changes that would keep errors from happening at all.

Her hospitals wouldn't wait for a death or major lawsuit to signal they needed to do something differently. They would begin tracking errors when they were small and creating solutions proactively. But human nature being what it is, she understood the hospitals would first have to take the stigma out of reporting someone's mistake by making it okay to make a mistake. Today, by every measure, this CEO's hospitals have far fewer errors.

Making it okay to make mistakes pays big dividends. When a prototype missile launch went wrong, rocket scientist Wernher von Braun gave a bottle of expensive champagne to the engineer who fessed up. "I may have inadvertently caused a short circuit," he admitted immediately, saving the team hours of retracing their steps and expensive redesign efforts. In the early days of IBM, when a newly promoted executive lost a lot of money on a bet that went wrong, founder Thomas Watson let everyone know he wasn't going to be fired. "Why would I fire him?" he asked. "We just spent thirty thousand dollars educating him."

Next, it's time to figure out who goes and who stays.

KISS A LOT OF FROGS: ACTION PLAN

▶ Let go of the fairy tale. Remind yourself you have to kiss a lot of frogs to find a prince.

▶ Build a culture in which every worker understands and believes that every little piece of innovation or reinvention is going to add to the company's ability to compete and grow long-term.

▶ Make as many small bets as your financial resources allow, with enough time available to analyze and learn from each one. A culture of change gets built by constantly making small bets.

▶ An added benefit of small bets is that incremental revenue often drops straight to the bottom line. The revenue generated by Starbucks' many small bets was greater than the company's total profits in 2010.

▶ Learn in loops by constantly changing, tweaking, improving, and improvising the small bets you make. Make your small bets SMART bets: Specific, Measurable, Accountable, Resourced, and Timed.

▶ Don't allow skunking—the spraying of negativity will ruin your small bets.

▶ Give good feedback—instruction that is relevant, helpful, and timely, in doses small enough to swallow—instead of waiting until it's too late to affect the outcomes or offering vague encouragement/pep talks that just frustrate the recipient. Get some feedback on the value of your feedback.

▶ Admit and learn from the mistakes you make. Mistakes are okay; the cover-up isn't.

CHAPTER 5

CHAPTER 5

WHO STAYS, WHO LEADS, WHO GOES

The right people are your only asset.

Ten years ago I was speaking to an audience of HR directors and began by asking them a question.

"How many of you are truly able to say you have a place at the leadership table in your company?"

Only a smattering of hands went up.

In the fall of 2011 I was speaking at another human resource strategy conference and asked the attendees the same question.

"How many of you can truly say you have a seat at the leadership table?"

Ninety-five percent of the people in the room raised their hands.

I couldn't help but smile as I realized what a difference the period between 2000 and 2010 had made!

The preceding story isn't about the growing importance of the role of HR; it's about the importance of people finally becoming acknowledged.

In the past decade there's been a change of epic proportions as most business owners and executives have come to understand that they don't stand a snowball's chance on a hot day of ever embracing change and growth without the right people who are focused and motivated every day at every level.

Buildings and plants don't matter, because anyone can build them; processes and efficiencies don't count, because they can be copied; and anything that any company makes, sells, or produces will eventually be done better, faster, and cheaper by someone else. Wall Street shows evidence of this change: Tangible assets were worth 62 percent of the typical NYSE valuation in 1982. By 2000 those assets totaled just 15 percent of the market value, a drop of 75 percent; and by 2010 most companies' tangible assets made up less than 10 percent of their value.

Decisions about who goes and who stays, who leads and who follows will determine any enterprise's ability to embrace constant change, growth, and reinvention. Making the right decisions about people is a huge challenge.

"All of a sudden," says Dan DiMicco, CEO of Nucor Corporation, America's largest steel producer, "all the experts are saying that people are your most important resource, and I like to point out to them that they're dead wrong. When I tell them that people aren't a company's most important resource they go, 'You can't say that, that's heresy!'"

"I let them argue with me for a little while," says DiMicco, who loves a challenge and a laugh, "and then I tell them what I really think. People aren't your most important resource—the *right* people are your only resource."

DiMicco says that no company should ever simply hire bodies. "Without the right people you will never achieve optimum success. The right people are those who take the initiative to get things done, who make things happen and whom you come to count on for ideas for constant change and improvement. A lot of people want to be taken care of in life, and they are never going to be or become drivers in your business," he says. "And they won't be good teammates either."

DiMicco and Nucor feel so strongly about finding the right

people that the company has a ninety-day trial for all workers. "Upfront we tell everyone," DiMicco says, "that there's a ninety-day period during which time they get to decide if they want to stay with us and we get to decide if they're the right fit for Nucor. During that ninety-day period they learn what we're all about, what they're really getting into, and the way everyone is treated, and we provide them a lot of feedback, but during that time we can also just tell someone, 'Sorry, it's not working, good-bye.'"

WHO STAYS (AND WHO GETS HIRED)?

Companies committed to constant radical change and growth recruit and retain workers who exhibit the following six traits:

Basic Smarts and Eager Lifelong Learners

Recently, I interviewed Brian Gale, the CEO of a midsize company in Cleveland that prints tags and labels. I asked him the same question I ask every business owner and leader I speak with: "What about your business is keeping you awake at night these days?"

He didn't hesitate with a response: "Without question my biggest challenge is finding the right people."

His answer surprised me, because the unemployment rate in Cleveland was hovering higher than 10 percent, so I prodded him a little more. "Why is it so hard to find people when the unemployment rate is so high?" And I added, "I'd guess that you'd have people banging on your door."

"There's no shortage of people applying for jobs," he said. "The problem is the quality of the people who are looking for jobs, and I'm never going to fall in the trap of just hiring a body for the sake of filling a spot," he went on to explain.

"As part of our application process," Gale said, "job seekers are given a short math test of ten questions. The first question is, 'There are one thousand labels on a roll and four rolls in a case. How many labels are in a case?' The past week," he said, "about twenty people have applied for jobs and taken the test, and almost all of them failed, including folks who'd graduated from community colleges. There's no way I'm taking a chance on any of them," he concluded.

There are a wide variety of assessment and evaluation tools available, and you should use them to make certain that someone possesses not necessarily a formal education, but sufficient intelligence to play a role in an organization that's going to call for nonstop learning.

But basic smarts are just half of the necessary mind-set. The second half is the ability to learn new things, something a surprising number of people find incredibly difficult.

Stanford professor Dr. Carol Dweck has been watching the behavior of bright people and how they learn since she was a sixth-grader in Brooklyn. Her teacher, Mrs. Wilson, ranked her class by IQ scores, and only the best were given the prestige assignments. Dweck noticed that many bright students were afraid of taking another IQ test, "because they might not be near the top anymore." That led her to pursue a career in psychology analyzing the way bright people see setbacks and how that profoundly influences their capacity for learning.

What are Dr. Dweck's conclusions? People who must look good to others, people who think mistakes make them look bad, and people who have "issues" with accountability or are so desperate they steal credit from others have a hard time learning new things.

You need to interview to understand how your candidates view setbacks. Do they avoid challenges and accountability for mistakes? Are they deeply concerned with how they look to others? How recently have they accepted a setback and learned something new? Can they give others credit for their success or are they stingy? Are they lifelong learners?

Answers to questions like these tell you a lot. If a person acts like he believes "Mistakes mean I'm stupid" or "The manager has to be the smartest person in the room," he will have a very hard time learning in an organization focused on constant reinvention. Plenty of bright and experienced people have a hard time learning new things.

The late Ken Iverson, credited with originally leading Nucor down the path to constant change and innovation, frequently used a saying still invoked daily at the company: "Anything worth doing is worth failing at." Nucor, which doesn't have an R&D department, is willing to try any worker's idea and see if it works. If it doesn't work out, the company figures out what it learned from the attempt and moves on without recriminations, long faces, punishments, or embarrassment.

A Good Work Ethic

In 1996, as part of a layoff, James Archer was let go from his job selling and supplying the chemicals to oil companies that allow them to effectively pump crude oil from the ground. He was thirty-eight years old and could have looked for another job, but it had always been his dream to build a company committed to doing things right, with high values and a workforce that wants to make a positive difference in the marketplace.

According to Archer, he found someone willing to lend him fifty thousand dollars in start-up funds with his IRA as collateral (which isn't technically allowed), and he began hitting the oil fields and making sales calls. Whenever he found someone willing to meet with him, he'd analyze their specific needs, order the chemicals he needed for a solution, and then mix up the final product in batches in the family garage. In only fifteen years he's built Multi-Chem, a company that does nearly four hundred million dollars in annual sales with its sights on the one-billion mark.

When he'd been in business for two years Archer decided it was time to hire his first employees and knew exactly the type of people he was looking for. "You have to hire people with a strong work ethic. They have to align with your values and they have to have integrity," he says, "otherwise you'll never be able to build a great company that thrives on change. We're willing to train and develop people, but if they don't have those traits it's a waste of time."

"The moment we hear someone start whining, 'Y'all work too hard . . . this business is too fast . . . all y'all do is work all the time,' we know we made a mistake and hired the wrong person, and we quickly help them find work with someone else. They can't be here to take part in our journey," says Archer.

Having a good work ethic means taking the initiative to get the job done, delivering as agreed without excuses or blame, being will-ing to make personal sacrifice for the good of the organization, and being loyal to the company and people with whom you work.

Nobody gets hired at Multi-Chem without taking a DiSC assess-ment, which is designed to measure an individual's dominance, influ-ence, steadiness, and conscientiousness within specific situations. Then, it's on to the cultural interviews.

One of the questions Multi-Chem asks during the cultural inter-views is, "What would you do if your boss told you to take four hundred and fifty gallons of chemicals to a customer but to write down that you'd delivered five hundred?" Archer says he's constantly amazed at the large number of people who say, "Well, if my boss told me to do it, I'd do it."

"That's the wrong answer," says Archer. "Integrity is what you do when someone isn't looking, and anyone who gives us the wrong answer doesn't move along in the interview process."

Applicants for a position at Multi-Chem are interviewed a minimum of five times by five different people in an effort to make certain the candidate has a strong work ethic and is a cultural fit for the company.

Archer believes that if you hire hard you're able to manage easy. "When you hire someone with a strong work ethic, who shares your values and fits your culture, you don't need a lot of rules or bureaucracy," he says. "All the rules you find inside most companies are there for the two percent of all people who don't do the right thing, and in the process of having rules for them they adversely affect the other ninety-eight percent of all people who don't need rules. It's a lot easier to not hire those two percent."

One of the markers of a good work ethic is conscientiousness. People who show you they are careful, thorough, organized (even a little obsessive), persevering, and achievement oriented are demonstrating that they are highly conscientious. In more than a hundred behavioral studies conscientiousness has reliably predicted better job performance across a wide range of jobs.

They Truly Like Your Company and Want to Climb Some Mountains

Jorge Velarde is Multi-Chem's VP and CFO. A former SVP of finance for the world's largest international Coca-Cola bottler, he first met with Archer when Multi-Chem was planning an acquisition, to see if he could help the company. Velarde noticed that Archer was utterly buried in paperwork and asked him, "If you had the time, what would or should you be doing?" Archer responded that he should be in the field with customers and employees, growing the business, and it was quickly decided that Velarde would come on board to handle the inside so Archer could do what he does best: constantly grow and reinvent the company.

"A few years ago," says Velarde, "we had a low-performing area of the company, primarily because of high employee turnover, which is a killer during high growth. That's when we incorporated doing multiple cultural interviews into our hiring process and immediately decreased turnover significantly."

James Archer laughs when he talks about the cultural interviews and says that not long ago he was asked by someone who'd been interviewed multiple times by the company whether they were ever going to offer him a job or just keep interviewing him. "Hire hard . . . manage easy," Archer reminded himself.

Like Dan DiMicco describes Nucor, both Archer and Velarde describe the culture of Multi-Chem as being a journey and not a destination. "Our culture is about climbing a mountain," they say, pointing out that "any mountain climber will tell you it's not about reaching the top: It's about the journey, overcoming doubts, bravely going into the unknown. It's about accepting your constraints without letting them overcome your goals." Archer describes it as "being driven by the thrill provided by a constant, never-ending journey with lots of accomplishments along the way."

Don't be naive, though. As great as it sounds in theory, many people really don't like journeys without a final destination. Fifteen years ago a general manager in the automotive business was telling me his story and got to the present, where he was doing so much work to satisfy customers that he was exasperated. "When does it end?" he asked me, pleading for some break in this crazy (to him) world of constantly growing customer expectations.

Optimistic

Companies that are committed to nonstop change and growth have no place for people who aren't able to imagine and see the possibility of better results tomorrow despite the problems and challenges of the moment. You need to look for people who are optimistic by nature instead of pessimistic.

Successful reinventors are a lot like the four-year-old boy on the farm whose parents found him one day playing in a pile of manure and gleefully shouting, "With all this horse poop, there has to be a pony in here somewhere!"

The right people are like the little boy in the pile of manure. They will adapt, improvise, and overcome challenges because their view of life is such that when they see a pile of horse poop they think there could be a pony in there somewhere.

Think Like the Owner

"One of the things that make us different than other companies is that our people think and act like the owner," proclaimed Charles Koch, the owner of Koch Industries, the world's largest privately held company. That's a big claim to make when you employ seventy thousand people in sixty countries around the world. I had to pause and consider his words for a moment, because in all my research I've never found an organization that large that was able to get everyone on the same page.

Koch Industries, based in Wichita, Kansas, is involved in hundreds of businesses, including refining chemicals, pollution control, minerals, ranching, fertilizer, and commodity trading. Since 1960 the S&P 500 has grown eightyfold. Using the exact same assumptions, the value of Koch Industries has grown 2,700-fold. In the past five years the company has invested nearly fifty billion dollars in acquisitions and capital expenditures and has reinvested 90 percent of its earnings into the company each year.

The company thrives on constant radical change, and every business unit is held accountable for two things: being a good steward of capital and creating authentic value for all the stakeholders. As long as those two things occur, the company remains committed to the business. But if a business unit stops creating value or being a good steward of capital, the unit is either sold, shut down, or given away. In the past decade Koch Industries had businesses as diverse as animal feed, coal mining, pizza dough, and trucking. The company constantly searches for and embraces potential disruptive innovations and invests in them. Its recent bets include renewable, clean, alternative energy; green chemistry and additives; pulp and paper; and textiles and fibers.

When I challenged Koch and asked him how it's possible to get everyone in an organization as large as his to think and act like the owner, he perplexed me even further by responding, "Getting people to think and act like the owner is the easiest thing in the world to accomplish, and it doesn't require legions of consultants or major transformations."

Seeing a look on my face that signaled either cynicism or a total lack of understanding, he explained further.

"You can't expect people to think and act like owners," he said, "unless they understand how what they do creates economic value. And when people are taught how they not only create economic value but that it's constantly measured and evaluated and that they stand to share in the profits, then thinking and acting like the owner becomes very easy."

They Belong Here

It was a very hot and humid summer evening in Minneapolis, and downtown was pulsing with tens of thousands of excited, mostly young people attending the Microsoft Worldwide Partner Conference. The leadership team who'd hired me to do a speech the next day wanted to get together at a downtown restaurant, and it turned out to be so jammed that we ended up knocking knees while sharing a tiny table outside on the sidewalk.

Seated around the table with me were the woman who now runs the company in Thailand, the then head of Microsoft's worldwide system builder channel, and the then VP of the company in Asia. After I'd answered their questions it was time to turn the tables. "You folks know about me because you hired me and say you've read my books, but I don't know anything at all about you," I said. "Tell me your stories and what brought you to where you are." There was a brief silence and it didn't appear that anyone was going to jump in, so I nodded at the VP of Asia, who was the most senior person at the table, and urged him to go first.

"My story is that I'm a total misfit," he laughed.

He guessed that it wasn't the start of the story I'd expected to hear from one of Microsoft's top leaders and continued. "Growing up, I didn't like sports, skipped school all the time, and the only things I liked doing were playing the piano and goofing around with computers. We weren't called geeks then but that's what I guess I was," he said. "I really didn't fit in."

At some point in our lives most of us have felt as though we didn't fit in. I couldn't wait for him to continue.

"I started and stopped college a bunch of times," he said, "but I was a horrible student and seldom went to class. I worked in a store fixing people's computers and played the piano in bars at night."

What he said next really surprised me.

"I had no plan and no idea what I wanted to do," he said. "I never even gave it a thought. I figured I'd be fixing people's computers and playing piano in bars for the rest of my life."

I listened intently, wondering how a guy without any aspirations had ended up with such a huge position and so much responsibility at the world's foremost software company. I had to prompt him with, "So, what's the road that took you to where you are today?"

"One day back in nineteen eighty-four," he said, "someone who'd heard I knew something about computers called and offered me a job at Microsoft and I took it," he said. "And almost as soon as I came on board, I knew I'd finally found a place where I fit in."

He told the story of how he'd quickly advanced from a sales job to a general manager position and within another couple of years earned his VP stripes. He'd then begun taking on incredibly complex roles for the company around the world before finally taking responsibility for all of India, China, Japan, Southeast Asia, Australia, and New Zealand.

"That's a neat story," I said. "I'd never have guessed that some guy playing the piano in a bar would become one of the top leaders at Microsoft." What he said next surprised me even more.

"You think *my* story is unusual?" he asked. "My story is nothing. In fact, I might be one of the more 'normal' people at the company."

And then he said something I've thought a lot about ever since.

"You have to understand that we're basically a company of misfits and people who didn't fit in anywhere else," he proclaimed. "That's what makes the company so great. We were all lucky to find *the* place where we belonged."

Steve Jobs frequently said, "Apple is an Ellis Island kind of company built on refugees from other companies. These are the extremely bright individual contributors who were troublemakers at other companies."

Nucor's Dan DiMicco jokes, "We drive to parts of the country where the radio signals fade out and say, 'Let's put another Nucor plant here.'" It's not far from the truth. But the plants are a magnet for incredible workers who like the Nucor way. I was surprised when I visited a plant in Utah and an hour before the shift change the parking lot was filled with employees clustered in small bunches and engaged in animated discussions.

"What's the deal?" I asked the plant manager.

"Oh," he said, "all the guys from all the shifts come in early every day."

"Why do they do that?"

"When their shift starts," he said, "they want to have their plan in place to produce more steel and make more money than they did yesterday." That explains how the plant, built to produce four hundred thousand tons of steel annually, by having the right people in place, now safely produces more than 1.1 million tons—almost triple its planned capacity—each year, and how Nucor steelworkers routinely earn more than a hundred thousand dollars annually.

If you have workers who don't possess the six preceding qualities it's time to do yourself a favor and do some serious housekeeping. Begin getting rid of them, and replace them with workers who have basic smarts and are eager lifelong learners, who have a strong work ethic, who want to climb some mountains with you, who are optimistic, who think like owners, and who act like they belong in your company. A workforce made up of people who share these traits will always be prepared for constant change and growth.

You should also ask the important question of who hired them and why, which brings us to the people who should be doing the leading in an organization committed to constant change and growth.

WHO LEADS?

The people chosen for leadership roles in companies committed to constant radical change and growth share all the previous traits and the following five attributes.

Good Leaders Treat People Well

"Outmoded, inaccurate, and a dangerous model of leadership." General Peter Schoomaker, the former commander of the U.S. Special Operations Command, minced no words when he criticized the conventional wisdom about hard-nosed top-down military leadership. "Army Rangers, Navy SEALs, Green Berets, Delta Force, Marine and Air Force Special Operations are expected to deliver creative solutions in ambiguous circumstances," the general said. "Strict commands from the top and grunts who obey without question and execute their orders just won't accomplish that mission."

Dan DiMicco is on the exact same page as Gen. Schoomaker. "Ninety-nine out of a hundred times when a leader doesn't make it at Nucor, it's not because they're not tough enough, not intelligent enough, or not technically strong enough. It's because they can't move off a command-and-control type of leadership. After six, twelve, maybe eighteen months, command-and-control leadership wears thin," he says, "and people end up resenting you. If you can't move off it, if you can't see the difference between being a boss and being a leader, you're going to fail."

DiMicco is the only guy in more than five thousand top-executive interviews who actually scared me when we first met, because he plopped me down on a chair in front of his desk and said, "OK, skip the BS and get right to it." He's got the body of a Green Beret, the focus of a Navy SEAL, and the command style of a general who earned his stripes battling on the front lines and at the tip of the spear. If I were a certain professor from the University of Chicago who has made a career out of arguing that "communication skills, teamwork, flexibility, enthusiasm, and listening skills don't correlate to managerial success," I'd keep that opinion to myself when in the company of Mr. DiMicco.

"You've got to be good at treating people the way Nucor people deserve to be treated, how we want them to be treated, and most importantly how they want to be treated!" DiMicco insists.

Good Leaders Are Good Communicators

"Leaders need to be a coach, a mentor, a disciplinarian, a salesman; to lead their team so that they accept change and take ownership," says DiMicco. Each of those jobs requires a good communicator.

If there's one thing I discovered that separates good communicators from poor ones it is that the best start by taking responsibility not for what they say but for making sure what they say is understood.

Joan Beglinger was named Nurse Leader by the Wisconsin Organization of Nurse Executives in 2009 for reinventing the leadership model at a big inner-city acute-care hospital in Madison, Wisconsin. She and her people achieved an incredible transformation that today attracts visitors from around the world. Critical to this success, Beg-linger told me, was turning the boss/subordinate communication model on its head. "The burden was put on us [the top executives]," she says. "We stopped thinking, 'Are they smart enough to get it?' We have to answer the question 'Are we good enough at communicating?'"

Then there's the former marine sergeant, now running teams in a technology company, who told me of the time when a corporal under his command forgot to process some necessary report. "I went to my lieutenant," he explained, "and told him *I* had failed to impress on the corporal the importance of getting that paperwork done."

Contrast the sergeant and Beglinger to Mickey Drexler, the one-time CEO of troubled retailer the Gap, who after a bad quarterly performance told the press, "I gave my people too much responsibil-ity. From today forward I'll be getting my mitts on the details and doing less delegating." In other words, "It's not my fault; my lousy team dropped the ball." Sometimes it doesn't matter how much cha-risma someone has if he's not a good communicator. By the way, he soon left for greener pastures.

A pitching instructor explained a bad coach as one "who says the same thing he just said a second time, only louder." Good coaches, in his mind, "have many ways to explain something so any athlete can understand. Performance is the acid test the communication was good." I don't think anyone ever communicated it better.

They Lead by Example

"We're looking for people who teach by example, not only verbally," Nucor's CEO explains.

Leopoldo Pujals, former head of Europe's Telepizza, told me that his secret for growing fast (from one location to one thousand in just ten years) was "proving the math." He learned firsthand exactly how many promotional flyers had to be passed out to sell the number of customers he needed each day, exactly what questions guaranteed customers got everything they needed with each delivery, and so on for every key performance activity required of a great store. Pujals could tell others what to do and what could be done because he had done it. And he grew fast because everyone who followed Pujals believed what he said—because they saw him lead by example.

CEO Fred Eppinger reinvented the Hanover Insurance Group leading by example. During his first week on the job he got rid of the regal head-office perks (private elevator, 24-7 chauffeurs, off-limits notices to nonexecutive staff, etc.) to announce "an open, frugal, and down-to-business approach. It also made a very clear statement to other executives, 'We're not going to be about trappings and executive privilege, but we will be about shared accountability for building something new and special.'"

Leading by example doesn't mean the manager is the best or first to do things, but it does mean that leaders who lead by example acknowledge what's really important and promote credibility, humility, accountability, and fairness.

All the reinventors lead by example. Jim Goodnight, CEO at SAS, still writes code; Joan Beglinger, VP in charge of nine hundred nurses, still puts on her scrubs and pulls bedside shifts; and Multi-Chem's James Archer calls on customers every week. As DiMicco puts it, "Unless you walk your talk, you have no credibility."

Build Trust

Doing what you say, leading by example, showing consistency and fairness—these actions all build trust between managers and their teams over the long term. But new managers often ask me if there's something they can do that builds trust faster so they can get more buy-in and can hit the ground running. Here's the good news.

A small but dedicated group of researchers in psychology, social anthropology, and behavioral economics has been studying trust over the past two decades. Trust, they have determined, plays a huge role in modern ideas about human evolution (getting unrelated groups to collaborate), mission-critical communications (coordination among diverse battlefield commanders), and even global business negotiation theories (different attitudes in the East and West about a laws-based versus trust-based relationship and its effect on profitability).

From their research we now have four guiding principles for building the early foundations of trust quickly:

▶ We trust those who speak our language.

▶ We trust those who ask good questions.

▶ We trust those who share our values.

▶ We trust those who listen.

All the leaders we interviewed for this book and my four other books have one thing in common: They come across (to even the most skeptical listener) as people you immediately trust. As I review thousands of pages of transcripts and replay the recordings of our conversations, I see those four guiding principles in action. They all talk without using MBA buzzwords and industry jargon, in simple yet compelling terms; they ask brilliant questions, showing an unquenchable natural curiosity; they share thoughts candidly, using life stories to illustrate what they value; and they are as interested as they are interesting, always listening with something I find quite uncommon in business, their *full* attention.

Attract and Keep Talent

Leading the Nucor way is critical to attracting and retaining talent.

It is called a virtuous cycle, that series of actions that when repeated builds tremendous momentum and will propel an organization to very positive outcomes.

Good leadership is a virtuous cycle at Nucor, explains DiMicco. "As leaders and managers we give our people the training, the tools, the resources, and the opportunity . . . and then get the hell out of the way and let people succeed. Now that attracts talent, the kinds of people who want to be able to do great things, want to benefit from their own performance and the performance of their teams."

Most notable in this simple equation is Nucor's insistence that once managers provide tools, resources, and opportunity they "get the hell out of the way." It turns out that the kinds of people who are quick to help an organization reinvent itself are creative, open, experimental, committed, and optimistic, and they won't tolerate micromanaging or bureaucratic nonsense. While all working people are annoyed by bureaucracy and micromanagement, the right people consider those two downsides of a big company a real deal breaker. So the first outcome of Nucor's virtuous cycle of leadership is better retention and keeping the right people. "It's as close to a zero-bureaucracy environment as you can find out there," DiMicco says.

The payoff shows in the metrics. The company's twenty thousand workers are the best paid in the industry, but the company has the lowest labor cost per ton of steel, leads the industry in return on capital, has the lowest financial leverage of any major steel company, and has paid 142 consecutive dividends. Retaining the right people sets up the company to do lots more with less.

Nucor's virtuous cycle pays off beyond retaining the right people. "Once we get into a community and walk our talk, word of mouth starts to spread and starts to bring in great people from other communities or from longer distances. Now the company is excelling still further, able to grow and reach new heights." It's a dizzying competitive advantage when you think of the money the organization saves.

While other companies are forced to pay fat signing bonuses and recruiter fees, sometimes going as far as acquiring a rival at a huge multiple of revenues—called acq-hiring—just to get some talent to fuel growth, Nucor has word-of-mouth affirmation attracting great people for a fraction of the money paid out by other companies.

"We found that we attract high-quality, motivated people who want to come back home [to smaller towns and rural settings in twenty-two states]." Nucor is in the locales young people left in search of better pay and better opportunities for their young families, but also the towns where they left Mom, Dad, aunts, uncles, cousins, friends, and neighbors behind. Now they can get the best of both worlds, coming back home to "jobs that pay three to five times more than average, a company that respects its people, is entrepreneurial and not bureaucratic, with a safe and secure future," DiMicco points out. "From the human resources side . . . it was a piece of cake!"

DiMicco wanted me to know that "it's not magic." And he's right; it's really common sense. But after a decade investigating a hundred thousand of the world's businesses and interviewing five thousand entrepreneurs, CEOs, and business owners I can tell you with confidence that the only thing common about this common sense is how uncommon it is.

WHO GOES?

If you have workers or leaders who don't fit the preceding criteria, they will slow you down and confound you in your efforts to create an organization that embraces constant change and growth.

Add up the countless time and resources that are utterly wasted by having the wrong leaders recruiting and hiring the wrong people. Then, fix the people thing and get the right leaders and workers on board, and constant change and growth will become your culture and will be achieved.

Once you've got the right people in place, the next big challenge will be keeping everybody on the same page.

WHO STAYS, WHO LEADS, WHO GOES: ACTION PLAN

▶ Acknowledge that the *right* people are the only asset that gives your business any value. Anyone in the organization who fails to enthusiastically buy into this belief and practice it should be immediately shown the door.

▶ No one is worthy of leading without possessing the attributes of treating people well, being a good communicator, leading by example, readily building trust, and having a track record of attracting and keeping the right people. Until you get the right leaders in place, your efforts at change and growth will be stymied.

CHAPTER 6

CHAPTER 6

GETTING AND KEEPING EVERYONE ON THE SAME PAGE

"Ours was a 'bid and quibble' business. We'd say this; they'd say no. We'd go back and forth and at some point end up at a place neither was happy about. We don't do that anymore."

—Larry Pope, CEO, Smithfield Foods

You know what it's like when everyone is on the same page, don't you? Work is more fun, morale is high, and when one workday ends people look forward to the next one.

When everyone's on the same page, teams get lots done without anyone barking orders or breathing down their necks, hard work isn't as draining, and sacrifices aren't a big deal. Problems get solved without too much fuss, but not because everyone always agrees. It's just that everyone does their best to communicate and cooperate, discussing any temporary rift like adults and coming to consensus quickly.

The beauty of having everyone on the same page is that it doesn't matter who is on the team—aggressive people, collaborators, creative types, bean counters, senior execs, front-line workers, old hands, or new hires—the most diverse groups overcome any obstacles and maintain their momentum.

Over and over the leaders we've interviewed have candidly shared the obstacles faced in their reinvention. Each time they successfully cleared those hurdles, the backstory included incredible morale, which made it easy for everybody to maintain their momentum.

In contrast, during the times when people were not on the same page, one could sense the dysfunction coming. The leaders' stories were full of people dragging their feet or sitting on their hands, chronically complaining and pointing fingers. Negativity and inertia were in the air, with associates working behind the leaders' backs to sabotage any follow-through or buy-in.

I received an e-mail recently that painted that bleak portrait in which none of the leadership was on the same page:

> I have a client right now where half of the executive team including the COO, the CTO, and the head of HR openly undermines the CEO. They create gossip and discontent among their direct reports and the middle management. They don't like, respect, or support the CEO, his mission, or his values. They don't want to leave because of their great stock options, so they stay and create dysfunction. The CEO suspects this but he won't make a move because he doesn't want to lose half of his top team. What he doesn't realize is he's already lost them.

Conventional wisdom says that if the destination is clear and the financial incentives are aligned you'll get people on the same page. But, as the e-mail I received demonstrates, conventional wisdom is frequently wrong. Leaders need skills beyond communicating the reasons for reinvention and explaining the incentives for success. They need to connect with everyone at every level—stakeholders both inside and outside the organization—understand their agendas, and get them all on the same page.

Consider the following somber numbers about the current state of affairs between workers, vendors, customers, and their bosses and companies.

American Business:
Not on the Same Page

Study after study shows we're not on the same page:

▶ 77% of workers don't trust the CEO and 61% don't trust any senior manager.

▶ 55% believe their company routinely "spins" the facts.

▶ 51% feel actively discouraged from challenging the status quo at work.

▶ 70% find the most stressful part of their job is dealing with their bosses.

It's no better between companies and their best customers:

▶ 55% would fire their enterprise software supplier if they could.

▶ 66% of organizations are sorely disappointed with their choice of outsourcing partners.

▶ 80% are ready to ditch long-term retail relationships today.

CNN / Gallup Poll, Watson Wyatt Work (USA) Study, 2002 and 2009, Towers Perrin, International Survey Research, *New Scientist* magazine, Gartner, PA Consulting Group, McKinsey Research

WHO'S RESPONSIBLE FOR GETTING EVERYONE ON THE SAME PAGE?

The day had been like every other day that week for the young management consultant—long, hard, and exhausting—and as the week wore on he'd been spending a lot of time thinking about all the disadvantages he faced, including a bad economy, customers who didn't believe in spending money to train their people, and associates who didn't seem as committed as he was.

Little did he know he was about to learn a lesson that would change his career and life forever.

He was in a California restaurant having a conversation with his client's much older (and wiser) COO, discussing how frustrated he became whenever he measured where he was in his career versus where he'd like to be.

The COO kept silently nodding in acknowledgement as he listened to the man vent, and then he reached for a cocktail napkin, took out a pen, and said, "Let's make a list of everything that's holding you back. What would you say is the biggest obstacle you face?"

"Well," the younger man began, "a new business like mine always has a rough time gaining credibility with older clients."

"OK," the COO said, and jotted a note: "credibility is number one."

The young consultant quickly added, "A lot of the things that would get me ahead cost more money than I can afford."

"So, money is number two," the COO said, writing it down. "What other things?" he asked.

The conversation continued and the writing on the napkin grew to include the other things that were holding the young consultant back from achieving his full potential.

Finally, the COO stopped his young friend. "I'm looking over your list and it's very comprehensive," he said. "You've obviously given this question a lot of thought. But I see that one thing is missing from the list."

"What's missing?" asked the young consultant.

The COO paused, looked his colleague straight in the eye, and said, "Your name isn't on the list!"

In other words, he was telling the consultant, "You are responsible."

That young consultant was me.

No matter how good your plan for change and growth is, it's going to run into some obstacles. How formidable those obstacles are will depend on your perspective. If you lay your head flat on the ground and look up at an anthill it can seem insurmountable.

The way you look at a problem may be a big part of the problem.

The best way to deal with the hindrances and obstacles you're certain to confront is to get and keep everyone on the same page, including your workforce, your customers, your vendors and suppliers, and the people who've made an investment in your enterprise or provided you with the capital required for growth. Don't forget, you are responsible for getting everyone on the same page!

WATCHING SAUSAGE GET MADE

The unconventional lessons of reinvention in this book have come from some very unusual sources, but no story was harder for me to get my head around than the reinvention story of pork producer Smithfield Foods. This company is like many that have faced constant obstacles confounding their commitment to growth and change. But it solved them through a most unconventional process, working relentlessly to get everyone, including their most damning critics, on the same page.

Smithfield Foods was founded seventy years ago when Joseph Luter Sr. and Joseph Luter Jr. opened their pork-packing plant in Smithfield, Virginia, to butcher and process hogs.

The company's original claim to fame was its unique hams, butchered and processed from pigs that grew fat and tasty on peanut vines in the Virginia countryside. Under the direction of Joseph Luter Jr., who became CEO when he was twenty-seven, the company remained a small but prosperous business, selling its products in Virginia and surrounding states.

After having enjoyed modest success for many years as a small regional company, Smithfield was acquired by a huge conglomerate with big plans, which within six years had essentially bankrupted the company. Luter, the former CEO, was asked to come back, take the reins again, and save the company. Upon his return the company was doing only twelve million dollars in annual revenues, had seventeen million in debt, and had a negative net worth. The experts said the company couldn't be saved.

Luter was determined to grow the business, and as soon as he'd stabilized the balance sheet he developed a plan for change and growth that would also solve one of Smithfield's big competitive disadvantages to growth: a bad location.

Being based in Virginia had originally provided Smithfield an advantage in terms of being able to get its fresh products to the big population centers on the mid-Atlantic coast with very low freight costs. But the reason most U.S. meat production is located in the Midwest is because the primary foods for meat are the grain and corn grown there.

Eventually, Smithfield was trucking millions of hogs from the Midwest to Virginia, and Luter realized that if he was going to significantly grow his company he needed access to all that Midwest grain and corn. He embarked on a buying spree that ultimately resulted in acquiring twenty-five other companies, literally taking over the Midwest and taking the company national.

The roll-up continued throughout the 1990s, as Luter purchased every large pork producer he could get his hands on. Always opportunistic, Smithfield bought other large producers and packagers when they got into financial trouble. By driving down costs and centralizing as many functions as it could, the company gained prowess in taking over companies with historical profit margins of 1 percent and doubling them to 2 percent or a little better.

Going from a margin of 1 percent to 2 percent might not sound impressive, but it's still a 100 percent improvement; the company quickly became a darling of Wall Street and one of the top twenty stocks to buy and hold for the past twenty years.

Having moved from being a small pork processor to the biggest producer and processor in the nation set the stage for Smithfield's next reinvention. Besides being a Wall Street favorite, the company had also made fierce enemies and earned the wrath of environmentalists and animal rights activists along the way.

Larry Pope, Smithfield's current CEO, is a native Virginian who joined the company thirty years ago as a controller. During his time at Smithfield he moved from controller to VP of finance and finally CFO before being named CEO in 2001.

"When I was about to take the reins," Pope says, "our chairman said to me, 'Larry, I've been the entrepreneur who grew this company; now it's your turn to professionalize it and then the next step will be to turn it into a marketing company.'"

"I realized how right he was," says Pope. "We couldn't continue to grow and do the same things we'd done in the past. We'd acquired everything we could, found ourselves with about a thirty percent market share bumping up against the wall from an antitrust stand-point."

"The entire industry had matured," he says. "All the farms and processors were big and efficient; there weren't any inefficiencies left to take out, and when that happens [in any industry] what you end up with is a commodity, and the only thing you have to talk to your customer about is how low your price can go. When you allow that to take place," he says, "you can kiss your margins and your financial performance good-bye. We knew we had to become the next Oscar Meyer, Sara Lee, or Kraft, and that was going to require lots more radical change."

Pope adds, "Plus, we're in a business lots of people don't like. We kill animals to put food on the table. It sounds terrible. I decided the only way to go forward was to do the right thing. We were going to be an ethical company. We're going to take care of our animals. We're going to take care of our people. We're going to take care of our products. We're going to take care of our environment. We're going to take care of our communities. We're going to change people's opinions and be proud of our company."

START WITH YOUR FIERCEST CRITICS

There's a man named Dennis Treacy, who has a framed first page of a lawsuit hanging on his office wall that reads, "Dennis Treacy Versus Smithfield Foods." He filed the lawsuit against the company when he was the head of the Virginia Department of Environmental Quality.

Treacy, a lifelong biologist and protector of the environment, was the least likely leader to help reinvent Smithfield Foods. After all, he'd sued Smithfield in a companion action with the U.S. Environmental Protection Agency.

"I didn't know the company well," Treacy admits, "but I knew enough to know I didn't think much of them. I knew them as a violator I'd sued and who the EPA had sued. I believed they didn't get it—they were not acceptable to the Virginia Department of Environmental Quality, and everybody in my world had a negative view of Smithfield."

Today, Treacy is Smithfield Foods' chief sustainability officer and SVP of corporate affairs. Sound familiar? A company once vilified by a government official hires that official to gain his silence? Read on and you'll learn just how truly committed Smithfield Foods is to radical change and reinvention.

Treacy says that when he attended his first meeting with the company in an attempt to settle the lawsuit he had serious misgivings. "I expected to meet people killing animals left and right; pirates with tattoos and a deck of unfiltered cigarettes rolled up in their sleeves. It was not what I expected!"

Instead he found a group eager to get on the same page, pay the fines, and resolve any issues. When Treacy's term as head of the Virginia DEQ expired he received an offer he couldn't refuse. The new CEO, Pope, said, "Dennis . . . here are the keys to the front door. If we're doing it wrong, go fix it."

"How far can I go in terms of fixing it?" Treacy asked him.

"As far as you need to," replied Pope, and Treacy says that Pope has never told him to stop but has instead urged him to go even further.

Treacy did just that, developing industry-leading sustainability and environmental compliance programs as someone who had the authority to protect the environment at every plant and farm. Nine years later the company gets awards instead of fines.

Treacy's role has expanded to reach out to all of the company's harshest critics: humane societies, food safety activists, animal rights groups, workers' rights groups, NGOs (non-governmental organizations) of all sorts, even PETA. "I told Dennis to go and engage them," Pope says. "Don't run the other way; talk to them. Don't be defensive; show them all we're doing and share the facts. Listen to what people outside are saying and prepare programs to intercept these challenges. Sometimes you will satisfy them, sometimes not. They have a right to their opinion. But we're going to try and get on the same page."

If you're thinking that this sounds like corporate social responsibility boilerplate and are skeptical about good intentions from corporations, Dennis Treacy knows how you feel. At first he wasn't sure if he'd last "three hours or ten years." And Smithfield's front-line managers were skeptical too. The macho culture of meat companies has the kind of guys who might say, "Ethics, schmethics—forget about it, we need to get chops out the door!"

Treacy explains what happened to change their views. "When you're able to align sustainability with good business sense—animal welfare, worker safety, environmental protection, etc.—and save a hundred million dollars a year at the same time, eventually, everybody sat up and took notice. Now," he says, "we're all one hundred percent on the same page."

SHARED SACRIFICE

The years 2008 and 2009 were among the toughest that Larry Pope and the company ever faced. Pope had transitioned Smithfield from an entrepreneurial company to a model financial enterprise, cleaned up the environmental messes, and was on his way to turning it into a savvy marketing company when the Great Recession occurred. "On top of the financial meltdown," says Pope, "we also had a severe industry downturn because the price of corn tripled [thanks to America's sudden love affair with ethanol], and I'm on the record as saying that I lost two hundred good nights of sleep. I thought the hole we were digging was so deep we should go into the swimming pool business, but we're back delivering one record profit after another."

Pope's favorite phrase is, "You need to be present to win," and when the recession hit, he shared this message with his workforce: "We've got fifty thousand people who work for this company around the world and rely on us for their livelihoods, and we don't want to lay people off, so let's do what it takes to be sure we're present to win when we come out of this thing."

The first thing Pope cut was travel. "I asked the company to stop doing any travel that wasn't necessary," he says, "and knew that I had to set the example. We've got two jets because we have operations and plants all over, but I said, 'Park the jets,' and we put the pilots to work painting the hangars and maintaining the planes." Pope started driving to plants and staying at Holiday Inns. "Anything you ask your workers to do *you* must be willing to do," he says, "because the leader has the responsibility to set the example.

"People have a strong desire to be part of the solutions and are eager to rally around doing the right thing. It was amazing to me," says Pope, "that in thirty days we reduced our travel expenditures by fifty percent."

Along with the promise to not institute layoffs, Pope also went on record as saying there would be no salary increases or year-end bonuses until the company got out of the woods. "I told everyone that we had to cut everything that could be cut without sacrificing the quality of our product. People want to know what the goal is and have it communicated in a very simple way. Communicate the mission honestly, fairly, and compassionately, get everyone on the same page, and people will do the right thing." Pope says he didn't receive one single complaint about the freeze on compensation.

EVERY DIME COUNTS

"As part of reinventing the company we were going to zig while everyone else was zagging and made the decision to start getting out of the 'commodity' mind-set and start increasing our margins," Pope says, and he again proceeded to get everyone on the same page.

Many businesses share the mistaken belief that money coming in the door cures all ills, but Pope doesn't buy into that idea. "A lot of companies will do almost anything, including keeping their factories churning out goods at any price, hoping that at some point the money will catch up with them. It's called 'capacity utilization,'" he says, "and chasing capacity can only lead to eventual failure."

Citing the example of a manager who called him from Florida to tell him the company was losing five cents on every pound of hot dogs they were selling, Pope simply told the manager, "Then we're getting out of the hot dog business in Florida."

The manager protested and said that hot dogs were fundamental to their business, to which Pope replied, "Losing money is not fundamental to our business, so we'd better start raising our prices."

Pope says that instead of settling for the industry's average four- or five-cent profit per pound of hot dogs the company decided to go for a profit of ten cents per pound and not sell any orders that didn't achieve that profit number.

Very quickly every salesperson in the company found a small plastic cube on his or her desk with a dime inside and the message, "I want my 10¢," and all the manufacturing people began wearing hats that proclaimed, "It's time for a Dime."

"It became a point of pride and a rallying cry for the company that our hot dogs were great and that we deserved to make a ten-cent profit per pound.

By getting the salespeople, marketing personnel, and manufacturing teams on the same page, Smithfield was able to stop doing business with customers with whom there wasn't a profit to be made and eventually got its profit margin to well over fifteen cents a pound.

SELL IT OR SMELL IT

The current radical change embraced by Larry Pope and Smithfield is turning the company into a well-known national brand.

"We're in a perishable business," says Pope, "and because we have to sell the meat or lose it, it's traditionally been a push business. Once we decide to butcher a hog we've made the decision that we're going to sell the meat, so if we can't find the right price, we keep lowering it until we reach a price point where somebody buys it.

"We're working relentlessly to get into a pull business where instead of one and two percent margins we'll achieve the four to eight percent margins enjoyed by consumer packaged goods companies, and we're making tremendous progress.

"As soon as we got everyone on the same page," Pope says, "and people understood that even if our volume initially dropped nobody would get their butt chewed out, we began rationing capacity, and everyone realized that our products were worth more than we thought.

"We were told we'd be thrown out of stores if we raised our price two cents," he says, "so, we raised it a nickel and didn't lose any volume. Then we raised them a dime, and found out that our brands are great brands. We'd been so afraid of losing a sale that we thought we had to accept any price the marketplace offered. We were afraid of our own customers. We discovered that in moving a company from a push to a pull business you have to be willing to say no to an order." It's a lesson lost at many companies.

Pope offers some sage advice for other companies and businesses wrestling with prices that have become or are becoming commoditized and want to change: "You can't do business today the way you were able to even a few years ago. You must have collaboration with your suppliers and your customers. This was a 'bid and quibble' business. We'd have a price; they'd say no. We'd go back and forth and at some point end up at a price. We don't do that anymore. We get on the same page.

"You need to have open discussions about costs and pricing with your customers and suppliers, and everyone has to be on the same page in terms of the need for everyone to make a fair profit," Pope continues, "or nobody will remain in business. Finally, we're reaching a point with our customers where they understand that if our products don't sell at a price that allows them to make a profit they should delist [stop doing business with] us. But the second part of that understanding is that our customers must never ask us to sell them our product at a price that's below our cost. Any company that wants to embrace change and prosper must have collaborative relationships with everyone."

THIS CHANGES EVERYTHING

No one argues about the value of having everyone on the same page. But our time in the trenches has many of us convinced it's an incredibly rare occurrence and maybe impossible. How else can anyone explain the state of our politics, with all the red state/blue state arguments that are like two flat screen TVs facing each other while playing opposing channels at full volume? It's just what happens in our diverse conversations—between generations, genders, religions, nationalities, ethnicities, and orientations. The number of people we can listen to and get on the same page with seems so very small. It's rare at work, at home, at the ballgame, and at the community center. We're far from being on the same page.

After talking to Larry Pope and the folks at Smithfield Foods, the penny dropped for me. We're not on the same page, and it's nearly impossible to get on the same page because we're going about it all wrong.

Pope says, "Don't run away, ignore, or pretend your critics are not there." Exhaustive research and simple observation show we subconsciously surround ourselves, in business and in life, with yes-men. It's apparent in our media choices, whom we socialize with, who gets invited to the strategy table, whom we ignore, and whom we take notice of. We seek evidence that proves we're right, and anything that suggests otherwise goes in one ear and out the other. I see it all the time in others, especially CEOs who are the last to realize how bad things are because the inner circle was protecting them from the facts. Now Pope has me seeing this in myself. Getting people on the same page starts with being open to these difficult conversations.

Pope says, "Engage your critics, and don't confront them in an argumentative way." We're taught in school to debate. We're taught to take a stand and use knowledge, skills, and cleverness to win converts and disable the other side. I remember in high school and university classes being asked to take a position out of a hat and then stand up and win the argument. I grew up good at winning, but looking back I see that I wasn't getting opponents on the same page. I was shutting them up with powerful advocacy. I'll bet you've seen the same thing from the outspoken in meetings and in conversation with your bosses. Getting people on the same page begins with getting rid of the need to always win the debate.

Pope also says, "Listen to them. They're not always wrong." This is where it all breaks down. We like to talk; we find listening to be hard work. I remember when CEO Tim Smucker told me that managers at J.M. Smucker are trained to "listen with your full attention." I thought, "Really? What's the big deal?" Then I thought about the eight hundred interviews I do each year and how I'm both energized and exhausted, sometimes dreading the next one. It can be like a cardio session in the gym. But Pope makes the workout even harder when he says of his critics, "They're not always wrong." What he's saying is the others that you must listen to aren't always talking through their hat or out the other end. For most of us, listening to opposing views, especially when those views are misinformed, is excruciating, like doubling the speed, incline, and time on the treadmill. Getting everyone on the same page requires putting effort into really listening.

Lastly, Pope upends our biggest tradition of all in dealing with others, especially those with different views. He says, "We made changes and implemented their suggestions."

Pope sees that keeping people on the same page takes total follow-through. "We told the groups though our action," he explains, "that we're not hard-nosed and [it isn't that we] don't care about what they think. We proved to them they have a voice and we ought to listen to it. And we know that if we're really listening we ought to react.

If they have a good suggestion we're going to implement it." Getting people on the same page means earning trust by doing, not by being charming.

SMITHFIELD'S ACCOMPLISHMENTS

It seems that Abraham Maslow was predicting the past decade of Smithfield Foods' reinvention when he wrote his findings on good leadership principles in *Maslow on Management*: "This is the path to success . . . not only because of the Declaration of Independence, or the Golden Rule or religious [ethical] precepts or anything like that but because this path leads to financial success."

Smithfield was the first in its industry to achieve internationally recognized success implementing environmental management systems and formalizing internal and external evaluation audits to protect and preserve the environment (measuring how they are increasing conservation, reducing pollution, improving animal welfare, and achieving sustainability).

The organization was recognized as one of *Fortune* magazine's "Most Admired Companies," won accolades from FTSE4Good (a UK-based group that measures environmental, human rights, sustainability, and ethical records of international publicly traded companies), received the first Supplier Sustainability Award given by McDonald's (including recognition for its animal welfare innovations), was called one of the "100 Best Corporate Citizens" by *CR* magazine, and received a Virginia Torchbearer Award in 2008.

Best of all, getting everybody on the same page has saved Smithfield Foods "a documented one hundred million dollars in costs," as Treacy notes.

The company has made everyone, including the skeptics, proud.

There are several tactics that will help you become much better at getting everyone on the same page.

Be Interested Instead of Interesting

I started my career as a radio talk show host in a small Midwestern city. Aided more by luck than talent, I quickly found myself in Detroit at age twenty-one, about to go on the air and host my first talk show in, at the time, the nation's fifth-largest radio market.

I was scared to death, and my nervousness clearly showed. Five minutes before airtime I sat fidgeting in the small glass booth, with a huge microphone and massive telephone console in front of me. In a glass booth next to mine the newscaster was doing the news, and I knew that within just minutes he was going to throw it to me, the microphone, and Detroit. My heart felt like it was beating a thousand times a minute; I was almost gasping for breath.

On the other side of the window, the midfifties, cool-as-a-cucumber engineer fiddled with his controls and suddenly spoke in my earphones so loud I almost jumped from the chair. "Are you nervous, kid?" he asked

"Ah yeah," I replied. "So nervous I'd rather not be here."

And then he said something I've never forgotten: "You'll be fine, kid. Just remember that when you have callers on the line you should be more interested than interesting. Let them be the show. You're just directing traffic."

Unfortunately, most people are so wrapped up in their own agendas and trying to accomplish what they have in mind that they won't allow themselves to be interested in others. When you take the time to truly listen to others and learn their story, where they're headed and what they're trying to accomplish, you'll find more opportunities to get on the same page and work together than you imagined possible.

It's not surprising that 87 percent of corporate buyers think salespeople don't understand their needs because they don't ask enough questions. The most common complaint is, "My rep talks too much."

Half of all managers admit "their new hires acted differently on the job than they would have predicted from their interview." Again, the most common complaint from interviewees was, "They weren't listening and they talked too much."

It's as though we're in love with the sound of our own voices. But this won't help everyone come together and make decisions that can propel the company forward.

Listen with Your Full Attention

The average speaker talks at a rate of 135 words a minute. But the average listener comprehends at a rate 400 percent faster. This means that when you are listening, your mind unavoidably races ahead of the speaker. You can't help but think other thoughts and sandwich in random observations as the speaker is telling you what she wants, thinks, or is concerned about. Your focus slips enough to routinely miss critical signals (an implication, a look of anxiety, or something subtle that changes the meaning of the word just spoken). That loss of focus causes you to ask the wrong questions at the wrong time and reach the wrong conclusions, making the dialog a lot less productive for you and irritating for the speaker.

The best way to maintain focus and stay in the moment of the conversation is to paraphrase and summarize as your conversation progresses. Take a moment to recall what she has said and restate it to her in a way that has her reply, "Yeah, I didn't use those exact words, but you got it."

The advantages are many—greater comprehension, tighter focus, better follow-up questions, and the signal to the speaker that you are really listening. As you read earlier, we trust those who listen.

Make Sense First; Make Judgments Later

We're all in a hurry. Every day we feel like we are responding to a crisis and that every delay is potentially deadly. We all rush to judgment. It's as if we're putting out the latest fire with no time to get the whole story.

Paul Gleason would say, "Not so fast." Gleason is remembered as one of the best wildland firefighters in the world. He led hotshot crews (diverse teams of multi-experienced firefighters) for two decades and battled more than five hundred major wildland fires. His specialty was mentoring emergency response leaders in methods to make better decisions in fast-changing, critical situations. His best advice was to get the whole story by making sense first and judgments later. "If I make a decision I tend to not listen. If I make sense I listen, and that may change my final decision."

He saw his judgments as "something you polish." You look for confirming evidence and get tunnel vision. Judgments close your mind in dynamic situations, and you miss important but subtle bits of information that are critical to success. In many instances Gleason believed that if the leader made sense he could let go and have the crews make their own decisions.

Listening with a wide-open mind will help you make sense. Add the words *to me* every time you think something doesn't make sense.

Saying, "That doesn't make sense *to me*," forces you to look for the rest of the story, the logic the other person sees in what he is saying.

Looking for the ideas (or concerns) behind the facts opens the mind and helps you make sense. The mother of modern management strategy, Mary Parker Follett, told of the time in a library when she sat shivering, wanting to close the open window. But the man sharing the room wanted the window open. She didn't argue or even suggest a fast compromise, such as closing the window halfway. She listened when asking him why he was so adamant. The bottom line was he didn't like a stuffy room. She found a solution that pleased them both (opening a window in a nearby room and creating better circulation) and made sense of the situation rather than a judgment.

Read Between the Lines

Think back to the last time you met someone for the first time at your child's school or at a cocktail party after an industry conference. Reading between the lines, you saw a lot—body language, choice of words, tone of voice, and any inconsistencies. One research project determined that the average person is able to make ten significant determinations about another person, from trustworthiness to educational level, without the other person even opening his or her mouth.

Dr. Heinz Kohut defined our ability to read between the lines as empathy, "the capacity to think and feel oneself into the inner life of another person."[*] It's our way of having reliable intuitions about the

---

[*] Heinz Kohut, *How Does Analysis Cure?* (Chicago: University of Chicago Press, 1984).

feelings, thoughts, and experiences of another without those feelings, thoughts, or experiences being communicated in an objective or explicit manner.

We all have great capacity for empathy. In fact, the inability to empathize is considered a disorder. All you need to do is amplify your natural empathy.

Richard Coraine, COO of the constantly reinventing Union Square Hospitality Group, has a recipe for increasing his organization's ability to read between the lines with customers and employees (one of his company's core competitive advantages). "Remember *The Wizard of Oz*," he explains. "The recipe for empathy is at the end. The wizard [about to leave Oz] says to the throngs of people seeing him off, 'Listen to the Scarecrow because of his brain, the Tin Woodsman because of his heart, and the Lion because of his courage.' Use your head, heart, and the courage to act. It's all you need to be great at reading between the lines."

GETTING AND KEEPING EVERYONE ON THE SAME PAGE: ACTION PLAN

▶ On a scale of 1–10, rank your workforce or team in terms of being on the same page.

▶ Have a representative and anonymous sample of the workforce or team rank on a scale of 1–10 whether the workforce is on the same page as the leadership.

▶ Figure out which steps need to be taken to get both numbers to a 10.

▶ Continue this exercise with your customers, vendors and suppliers, lenders, and investors.

▶ Ask yourself daily who is responsible for making these things happen.

▶ Remind yourself daily to spend more time being interested than interesting.

CHAPTER 7

FOREVER FRUGAL

Necessity is the mother of reinvention.

—what Plato should have said

In 1975 a small start-up airline was bleeding cash profusely. The company's first president and his VP of operations realized their new company was between a rock and a hard place. "Do we accept defeat or do we find a way to cut our expenses by twenty-five percent overnight?" they wondered.

At the time the airline had four aircrafts flying around three hundred flights a week. If they cut flights or destinations it would mean disappointing their new customers; if they ordered layoffs it would mean breaking promises to new employees. So the pair searched for another solution.

"If we could find a way to make three planes accomplish the work of four we could sell off one plane and still keep our commitments to both our customers and employees," the president, Lamar Muse, suggested. At the time, each of the airline's flights averaged fifty minutes in the air and twenty-five minutes at the gate unloading, cleaning, refueling, and loading again. When Muse crunched the numbers he found that "if we could cut our turnaround time by sixty percent [from twenty-five minutes to ten] we could keep our current schedule and even add nine more flights." The president asked his VP, "Do you think our teams could make these quick turns?"

"We can and we will," Bill Franklin, the ops VP, replied.

Over the next two days the ops team reinvented the ground operations while the chief dispatcher and Muse rearranged all the schedules. All the supervisors and employees pitched in, coming up with a plan to create greater cooperation and coordination from all twelve different job functions, which would have a critical impact on airplane turn times. Getting everyone from flight crew to baggage handlers to do whatever was necessary to meet a ten-minute quick turn goal was something other airlines had thought about but had decided was impossible.

By the end of the weekend, crew routings and assignments were rescheduled and everyone was on the same page. After several days of successful ten-minute turns of three aircraft, everyone was able to breathe a sigh of relief. They sold the fourth airplane and stopped the bleeding. The airline's cash crisis was averted, and profits soared from the increased productivity.

That's the real story about how a small, upstart airline reinvented itself, got a new lease on life, and prepared itself to fly high and become America's largest airline (in terms of domestic passengers). You now know them as Southwest Airlines.

Since those early days Southwest has reached the top of everyone's list of inspiring and innovative organizations. The airline is a global icon of high quality, superior customer satisfaction, unparalleled productivity, and total teamwork in an industry infamous for finger-pointing management and "it's not my job" employee attitudes that leave scores of customers dissatisfied and disloyal. Without a doubt founder Herb Kelleher's passion for building a people-focused culture was crucial to the airline's success, but imagine for a moment that back in 1975, instead of facing a cash crisis Southwest had deep pockets filled with venture capital. Its leaders may have never discovered the innovative solution to quickly turning airplanes based on coordination and cooperation among every job function, from pilot to gate personnel. The company could easily be a footnote in aviation history, like People Express, Skybus, and scores of others. "Not enough" money was certainly the catalyst, the mother of Southwest Airlines' first reinvention.

When companies haphazardly throw money at what they perceive their problems, challenges, and opportunities to be, the *real* answers that could solve the *real* problems or allow them to embrace radical change and take advantage of the real opportunities are seldom found.

Other U.S. airlines became outraged at the success enjoyed by Southwest, but rather than embracing radical change and dealing with an outdated hub-and-spoke flight system, obsolete labor agreements, and horrible morale as a result of the shabby way they treated their workers, they either threw money at lawsuits trying to squeeze Southwest (as did American Airlines) or tried to beat them at their own game with copycat subsidiary airlines such as United Airlines' discount carrier, Ted; US Airways' MetroJet; and Delta Air Lines' aborted Delta Express and Song. At the end of the day, none of their frivolous lawsuits stopped Southwest and none of their copycat tactics prevailed, as Southwest grew its number of total daily flights to nearly four thousand.

As a former CEO of United Airlines recently confessed to me, "The profits reported by airlines aren't all that great, but airlines have terrific cash flows, and great cash flows allow you to cover up and bury a lot of mistakes or problems."

The lesson is clear: Having too much money or too many resources can actually get in the way of successful reinvention.

THE DOWNSIDE OF DEEP POCKETS

Do you remember Boo.com? Boo was the dot-com dream of two photogenic twentysomethings, Ernst Malmsten and Kajsa Leander (he a poetry critic; she a fashion model). Malmsten and Leander saw themselves as experts of "world cool, world chic." Their big idea was to create a cutting-edge Web site and reinvent the high-fashion shopping experience with Planet Boo, a 3-D gateway to a virtual world of hip and trendy international sportswear labels for fashionistas and their followers here on planet Earth.

Bernard Arnault, the chairman of LVMH, Europe's largest luxury goods group; Alessandro Benetton, the Harvard-educated son of Benetton's chairman, Luciano Benetton; and Bain Capital and J.P. Morgan must have loved what they heard in the pair's venture pitch. Planet Boo was given deep pockets stuffed with almost two hundred million dollars of other people's money.

Leander, Malmsten, and their crew spent all that and a few dollars more in just eighteen months. Here's a short list of what they reportedly bought:

- $70 million in software and servers

- $42 million in advertising

- $200,000 to rent apartments for Leander and Malmsten, plus $100,000 each to redecorate their pads

- $600,000 to PR firm Hill and Knowlton

- $200,000 per month in travel expenses

- $5,000 a day in stylists' charges to perfect the look of Planet Boo's mascot, Miss Boo.

- ❱ $1,000,000 to design their magazine

- ❱ 400 people doing the work of 80

For all that spending, Boo's investors got a total of only a half million hits (videos of giggling babies routinely get more hits on You-Tube in just a few days), two million dollars in sales, and at final liquidation (months after the buying spree) a pathetic $962,000 for all the assets and goodwill. Boo indeed!

Companies with long histories of successfully embracing change and reinvention have a shared disdain for waste and indulgence, which probably comes from the fact that during their formative years they had to count on ingenuity instead of cash to maintain momentum and keep on creating better tomorrows for all the stakeholders.

THE UPSIDE OF NOT ENOUGH MONEY

Arrow Electronics is the quintessential example of what I've learned in thousands of interviews with successful entrepreneurs: "If you want to accomplish great things, what you need is a problem and not quite enough money." Arrow was once a very small business and is now a twenty-two-billion-dollar worldwide company that has constantly embraced radical reinvention and succeeded without a lot of cash.

The company began as a retailer with a single location. Realizing that their best opportunities existed in wholesale distribution, the leaders proved themselves adept time and again at letting go and discarding companies and business units that no longer fit the strategic direction of the firm. Arrow's reinvention efforts have been doubled under its current CEO, who promised that going forward the company will be involved in "everything that has an electrical part or component."

"Ours is a company that grew despite never having quite enough money," says Arrow CEO and chairman Mike Long. "Things were so tight that for many years we wouldn't allow our general managers to hand out payroll checks until after five p.m. on Fridays so that our employees wouldn't cash them until Monday, when we'd hopefully have money in the bank to cover them all.

"If you can do the things that customers need done but that are giving them fits, and you scale that, you'll be very successful. We know that if it's complex we can make money at it."

THE EARLY DAYS

Almost one hundred years ago, as radio broadcasting was first sweeping the nation, a huge market developed for new and used radios, places to get radios repaired, and stores that sold vacuum tubes, spare parts, and tuners to those early radio geeks who preferred to tinker and fix things themselves. Very quickly, many major U.S. cities had an area of their downtown that came to be referred to as Radio Row (much like Auto Rows today), lined with stores selling radio-related merchandise.

No Radio Row was as famous as the one on Manhattan's Lower West Side, on the site of the former World Trade Center, where hundreds of stores stood side by side selling their wares. The stores were so jammed with merchandise that pictures taken at the time reveal huge bins of parts spilling into the streets and scores of customers doing an early version of Dumpster diving, their bums in the air, rummaging deep in the bins for their needed parts.

In 1935 Maurice Goldberg opened Arrow Electronics as a small retail store on Manhattan's Radio Row. By the late 1960s Goldberg had two stores, an electronics distribution business, and a spot on the American Stock Exchange. Three men, Duke Glenn, Roger Green, and John Waddell, who'd become good friends while attending Harvard Business School, acquired a majority interest in the company, sensing a real opportunity in electronics distribution.

Among the skills Glenn, Green, and Waddell developed while studying at Harvard was how to leverage a balance sheet and rapidly grow a company using stock and very little cash to acquire other firms.

In a model not unlike that of Smithfield Foods, they'd find a company that they believed fit their long-term vision of electronics distribution and buy it using the shares of Arrow as currency. Then, they'd reduce the new company's operating expenses by eliminating any functions that could be centralized, while simultaneously doing whatever it took to grow sales, which resulted in improved growth for the entire company. Without coming up for air, they'd take their story of growth to Wall Street, leverage up, ID their next target company, and do it all over again.

During their first twelve years of leadership the three partners took the company into electronics distribution, licensed consumer electronics, audio speakers, and a dramatic expansion of their retail presence. The scrappy company earned a spot on the NYSE and became one of the top five electronics distributors in the nation.

In December 1980, tragedy struck when the top thirteen officers of the firm, including Glenn and Green, were meeting at Stouffer's Inn, in Westchester, New York.

Arrow's officers were conducting their annual budget-planning meetings at the hotel and on the spur of the moment asked the hotel for the use of a small conference room for an impromptu gathering of senior officers. Shortly after their meeting began, the entry to the room became engulfed in flames and the panicked group tried escaping through a set of doors leading to another conference room. What they didn't know was that the doors had been dead-bolted on the other side to prevent a decorated Christmas tree from tumbling over in the event someone accidentally opened the doors. All the attendees perished.

The subsequent investigation revealed the fire had been set by a hotel worker who feared he was about to be deported because of his illegal immigration status. He'd believed that if he secretly set the hotel afire and was then seen extinguishing it and saving lives, he would become a hero and not be deported.

Following the fire, John Waddell, the sole surviving partner and senior leader, spent his time assuring investors and reporters that Arrow could and would continue in business. He immediately brought in Stephen Kaufman, a former McKinsey and Company partner, to help rebuild the company's management team.

Kaufman, cut out of the same cloth as Waddell, served as a senior leader and then president and CEO until 2002, during which time the company made more than fifty acquisitions following Waddell's formula of issuing stock to finance the acquisition, keeping all the salespeople, and consolidating warehousing, management, HR, accounting, and finance. Arrow also left the retail business and made its first forays into the Asian and European markets, growing to twelve billion dollars in annual revenues and becoming one of the two largest electronics distribution companies in the world.

In 2003 Kaufman stepped down as CEO and Arrow recruited William Mitchell, a thirty-year veteran of the electronics industry, to serve as its president and CEO. During Mitchell's reign he focused the company's attention on Asia and continued an aggressive program of acquisitions. The company continued growing its revenues and became one of the two hundred largest companies in the U.S.

From the depths of the Great Depression through wave after wave of roll-up consolidation, one fact was constant: Arrow was always strapped for cash, yet it kept growing and growing.

MIKE LONG:
THE QUINTESSENTIAL REINVENTOR

When I'd finished writing the following profile of Mike Long, the CEO of Arrow Electronics, I decided it was too long and that I'd have to shorten the story and cut out any words or paragraphs that didn't specifically highlight a trait of a successful reinventor or teach a vital lesson about embracing change. To make my job easier I highlighted every character trait and lesson learned that has made Mike Long America's quintessential reinventor. In the end I didn't cut out any words.

Mike Long, Arrow's CEO, radiates the authenticity and humility you'd expect of a farm boy from rural Indiana. "Growing up a farm kid our family didn't have much money, but we sure ate well," Long says. At an early age his father told him that there were two things expected of him: working and playing sports. Both pursuits served him well.

As a teenager Long worked for a contractor, digging holes and hauling lumber, and during high school he learned enough carpentry that by the age of eighteen he'd started his own construction business. "It was the construction business and playing football for the University of Wisconsin that got me through school," he says. While most CEOs with a background in athletics cite sports as a key influence in their lives, it was Long's construction experience that taught him how to grow a business without a lot of money.

"I started my construction business without any money at all," Long recalls, "doing small jobs, odds and ends for people I knew who needed things repaired or built. The business did well, and I started getting work from insurance companies to fix homes damaged by weather, neglect, or fire—all the messy stuff that other contractors didn't want to do. The big lesson that taught me," he says, "is that if you're able to take the complex things that people don't want to deal with, get them out of their lives, and solve them, you can make some serious money without having a lot of money.

"When I graduated my dad told me that anybody could be a contractor and that it was time to go out into the real world and use my education and get a job." Long took a job as a buyer at Allen-Bradley Company (now a unit of Rockwell Automation) but quickly realized that being an hourly worker was a dead end and decided to become a salesman for the company. His efforts were rebuffed; he was told he needed an engineering degree to become a salesman for the company.

"After two years of night school studying engineering I decided I didn't want to be an engineer, that I'd mastered the basics, and I went back to the brass and told them I was ready to become a salesman, and again they told me no and said I had to have a full-fledged engineering degree." Long says that before that time it had never occurred to him to look for a job somewhere else; he'd assumed he'd be there for life. Out of frustration he applied for a sales job at Arrow, but the company also told him no, that he wasn't qualified.

Finally a company called Schweber Electronics, a specialist in the distribution of semiconductors and connectors, decided it needed a presence in Milwaukee and hired Long as a salesman to cover the territory. Schweber rented a five-hundred-square-foot office for Long, and he became the salesman, coffeemaker, and cleaner-upper.

"I took the job and ran," he says, "and worked harder than I'd ever worked to build the business, and it took off so fast that the company decided they needed to put a general manager in to manage the office, and the VP came up and told me they wouldn't give me the job because I was too young. I thought that was a raw deal and I let him know my feelings, and he obviously figured out I might leave, so one night about midnight I got a call at home from him. It was obvious that he'd been out drinking. He said, 'If you can be in Chicago tomorrow for a meeting at six a.m. we'll give you the job.'

"I got up in the middle of the night," Long continues, "drove to Chicago, and was in the parking lot at five a.m. waiting for them. Neither of them showed up until after ten o'clock, and when they did the VP said, 'What are you doing here?' and I told him he'd called me at home the night before and told me that if I could be in Chicago by six the next morning the general manager's job would be mine."

Avery Long, the slightly hungover VP, looked at his boss and asked, "Did I say that?'

The boss nodded and said, "Don't you remember? You called the kid at midnight and offered him the job."

Long says the rest is history. First he became a general manager, then they made him a vice president and eventually a regional vice president, but when Arrow bought the company, Long decided to leave.

"I wanted to move up the ladder," he says. "I wanted more responsibility and figured I didn't have a future with Arrow, seeing as how they'd turned me down for a job years before. So I went to the CEO and said, 'Look, I'm going to leave but I'll stay through the transition, make certain the good people stay, and then you can replace me with an Arrow executive.'"

The CEO asked Long if he'd interviewed with any other companies. He replied that he hadn't and wouldn't consider doing so until he wrapped things up with Arrow. The CEO asked Long to give him thirty days to come up with something that would broaden his horizons. "All I ask," the CEO said, "is give me the first shot at coming up with something for you."

"On the thirtieth day the CEO called me," says Long, "and told me he wanted to open a different kind of business, a business where the guys who would open it would have to put money into it alongside Arrow and that Arrow would loan the company money to grow the business. What Arrow wanted in return was the right to buy the business if things worked out. That's how Capstone Electronics got started," he says. "I took a mortgage on my house, put all my money into the company, and, as things turned out, the business boomed, Arrow bought it from us, and it was the first time in my life that I made some serious money and was able to pay off my mortgage, one hundred percent of my debts, and still have money in the bank."

Following the purchase of Capstone by Arrow, the company's CEO, Steve Kaufman, asked Long to move to Greenville, South Carolina, and fix a big problem that could potentially bring the company down. Arrow had purchased a computer and printer business and was losing money. Soon after his arrival Long realized that the company they'd acquired was in the wrong business. "The business was growing fast but there wasn't any profit in it," he says, "and I reported back that we could use the business as a foundation to get into another business and then sell off the computer and printer business."

When you spend any time with Mike Long, you quickly realize that one part of his brain is always mindful of the powerful lesson he figured out when he was running his contracting business: Find something that people and companies find complex and painful, come up with a solution to make the pain go away for them, and then figure out how to scale it.

"The writing was on the wall that there weren't ever going to be big margins in building and selling computers and printers," says

Long, "and a partner and I in Greenville figured out that we needed to move the business into something more complex." The pair used the business as a base to get into the server and systems business, which today represents Arrow's North America computer business and does more than eight billion dollars annually. According to their initial plan, they sold the original PC business to a company called Synnex, and it still exists today.

In 2008 Arrow finally named Mike Long as its CEO. He quickly made his vision very clear: "If it has an electrical or electronic component in it we're going to be involved."

Since Long took charge, Arrow has made as many as ten strategic acquisitions in one year. But more impressive than the sheer speed is his reinvention of the integration process, succeeding where other companies fail (seven out of ten times) and making those acquisitions pay off.

For example, in early 2008 Arrow acquired Logix S.A., a midrange IBM IT solutions distributor based in Europe. At the time, founder Laurent Sadoun had Logix on track to do about three hundred million dollars annually. Thirty-six months later Logix is fully integrated, with sales up 500 percent, over a billion and a half dollars a year.

This huge success is due to the reinvented acquisition process. And according to Mike Long the most important changes didn't cost an extra dime.

"We keep the entrepreneurs 'entrepreneurial.'"

Entrepreneurs like Laurent Sadoun have great qualities. They are highly creative, blessed with awesome gut instincts, are charismatic leaders, and possess the uncanny ability to attract scores of talented people and great customer relationships. That's because the very best don't do what they do just for money. They have a dream.

All entrepreneurs get strapped for cash. Private equity and other sources of funding will buy into the company. But many don't buy into the dream and end up driving the entrepreneur away. "We don't want to let that entrepreneurial dream disappear when they become part of our twenty-billion-dollar business," Long says.

"We keep the entrepreneur by letting them continue to grow the dream. Like every acquirer, we are buying them because there is something special about them that we believe can go the distance. But unlike so many other acquirers, we encourage them to take their dream the distance. If they are strapped for cash, need help with their balance sheet, need some synergies with other products, we've got their backs.

"Sadoun had his dream, and when we got together, our combined dream ended up bigger than any of us thought originally," Long explains. "We all got on the same page, and Sadoun became the principal architect. He helped us find other related acquisitions, and together we have built a business that does many more things than anyone thought when we first got together. And he's now leading all of it." Growing the dream and keeping entrepreneurs entrepreneurial has been one of the drivers of Arrow's success.

"We make everyone feel they're a part of it."

Acquirers often behave like conquistadors—throwing their weight around, disrespecting the natives, imposing foreign beliefs, and dealing harshly with anyone who dares to push back. Later these acquiring conquerors are dumbstruck when they are unable to get enough buy-in from the front lines to make their acquisition strategy succeed.

Long is different. "I haven't gone in and said, 'No! Do it this way, do it that way, do it my way.'" He positions Arrow to act like a bank, but with a really *cool* attitude, a bank that understands that the people are the ones who can grow a business fast. "We set targets and help scale the organization to reach an entirely different level. Then we let them execute."

Arrow doesn't allow that kind of "home office knows best" bureaucracy that kills momentum. "The people that run a business really know that business. We execute better because we push activities and decisions down to them," Long explains. "I believe our success is because the people we acquired in the deal all feel they are a part of it."

"We are ferocious learners."

"I hate to tell you," Long says candidly, "but we don't know where everything will lead.

"When we got into the computer business we had no clue what we were getting into, and our first year in the storage business we lost six million dollars. Some wanted to scale back. But I said, 'Look at all we are learning and if we add some costs in we'll be fine.' Today storage is worth north of one billion dollars and the computer business will approach eight billion dollars for us."

Strategy for both businesses (and the rest of Arrow) again follows Long's simple guiding principle: "If you can do things customers need that are giving them fits, and you scale that, you can be very successful." Learning what gives Arrow's 120,000 customers agita or pain has revealed the road map for leadership in a $150 billion industry. "Learning costs nothing, and learning pays big," Long explains. But at Arrow learning is a journey that will not end.

"I liken our journey to driving on a highway and visiting new cities. Every time you go to a new city you'll learn something, but in order for that to happen, you have to be on the highway. We don't know where every road will take us, but it won't take us anyplace unless we're on the journey."

If you want to embrace constant change and reinvention, you'd be wise to measure yourself against the character traits and life lessons learned by Mike Long and quickly figure out how to make them your own.

Long's assertion that the road to change, reinvention, and growth is determined by learning how to solve a problem that perplexes customers and then using persistence and knowledge to scale the solution would sound very familiar in India, where they even have a name for creative problem solving without a lot of money.

JUGAAD

Jugaad started as the Hindi word for an ultracheap vehicle first fashioned by rural Punjabi carpenters. Having nothing but empty pockets and a problem to solve, the local craftsmen took an old diesel irrigation pump, attached it to a wooden frame, and added wheels and the discarded steering system from a broken-down jeep. They called this jalopy "jugaad," roughly translated as "using few resources and a lot of determination to find an innovative solution to a problem."

Since then jugaad has come to symbolize the grassroots genius and entrepreneurial spirit of Indians working to overcome obstacles with creativity, urgency, and never enough money.

The best of jugaad is visible in the work of Ashish Shah's people at the GE Healthcare laboratory in Bangalore, India, where they've created a handheld EKG that fits into a backpack and costs just one dollar per patient to run a test. It's also in Ananth Krishnan's water purifier, which provides abundant bacteria-free water for only twenty-four dollars per household. Tata Motors' ultra-affordable twenty-two-hundred-dollar car, Godrej & Boyce's seventy-dollar battery-operated fridge, Anurag Gupta's smartphone ATM, and fifteen-year-old Remya Jose's creation, a pedal-powered washing machine that can clean seven pounds of clothes in minutes without electricity, are other great examples.

Indian businesspeople aren't the only ones to practice jugaad (think of the American phrase "Yankee ingenuity" or rural Sweden's principle of *lista*), but as a culture they have embraced this guiding principle with great gusto. Eighty-one percent of Indian businesspeople cite jugaad as the catalyst for their company's success.

Jugaad starts with the needs of a large population, such as safe drinking water, fresh food, the ability to get from point A to B, improved personal hygiene, etc. Next jugaad looks at existing products stripped of all bells and whistles, searching for simplicity. Finally it uses basic science and two-fisted ingenuity to fashion a solution in spite of limitations—little water, no electricity, tiny incomes, distant communities, and limited infrastructure. One can argue persuasively that it was the principle of jugaad that caused Southwest Airlines to come up with the solution of a ten-minute airplane turnaround or Arrow to acquire dozens of companies without much cash.

Ingenuity in product offerings is just the start. Jugaad also looks for waste in processes and business models. For example, thirty-billion-dollar mobile communications company Bharti Airtel Limited was the first cell phone company in the world to outsource everything but its customer relationship operations. It has achieved some of the lowest charges and highest quality (earning a Cisco Gold

Certification) in its industry by persuading partners to rethink their business models as well, getting network providers to charge by the minute and tower owners to allow the company to rent space rather than own it.

In an interview, former CEO of General Electric Jack Welch described his goal of "rethinking products from the customer perspective back to the factory." At the time, most manufacturers had a "move the metal" mentality, which meant that marketing and sales had to figure out how they could get customers to accept products and quantities—whatever the factory produced—even when they were not in their best interests. Welch's idea was to change that mind-set by putting the customers first in strategic planning and getting everything in sync with their circumstances and demands. He wanted executives to look at the supply chain and reverse engineer their strategies.

Executives at Walmart did just as Welch had suggested, disciplining themselves and their suppliers to work on "price-based costing" instead of "cost-based pricing." By ruthlessly rethinking, reengineering, and reinventing every little decision in every link of their supply chain, Sam Walton and his team created innovative new business models that delivered customers a much better deal.

Companies that successfully embrace constant change and reinvention must continually reexamine everything through the eyes of their customers, determine what customers are prepared to pay for a solution, and then figure out if they can earn enough profit to make it worth their while.

Like every good strategy in business, the lessons of jugaad can be misused. Some in India have used the concept to justify a "by hook or by crook" (illegal or unethical) attitude, as long as it gets the job done. That's been a problem with frugal and lean thinking for more than a decade. In the U.S., "Chainsaw" Al Dunlap and others like him paired lean with mean to suggest that they had a license as true capitalists to break commitments and hearts as long as it drove quarterly profits.

Our research shows that in contrast to these lean and mean managers, true practitioners of lean reinvention are the furthest thing from mean in thought, word, or deed. Many refuse to allow themselves the easy answer of layoffs and heartless leadership. They're tough and demanding, but they run their lean companies with fairness, principle, and integrity.

Mike Long says, "When the days were at their darkest and the economy was plummeting in 2008, we planned to do some layoffs. I was sitting across from one of my executives and said, 'If everybody from the two of us down to our regional level of executives would be willing to take a ten percent pay cut we could save *five hundred* jobs.' I floated the idea in a town hall meeting and didn't get any grimacing or grousing. We just didn't have a mentality that layoffs are good. We came to the conclusion that if we shouldered the cuts at the leadership level, when the economy turned we'd have five hundred people we didn't have to hire, plus we'd have people with the knowledge and passion to help us reach new heights fast. And you know what? They have!"

BEING FRUGAL SPURS REINVENTION

"Spending on scientific research is at an all-time low," a renowned pundit told his audience. "If one more dollar is cut I fear we'll create an insurmountable innovation gap." We hear a lot of that kind of talk in businesses and in government. We're facing tough times, and any cutbacks are quickly labeled self-defeating. But is that true?

IBM recently celebrated one hundred years in business. It also celebrated another milestone: one hundred billion dollars in worldwide revenues. Life is good at Big Blue—so good that it would be easy to forget that in the early 1990s this same iconic technology giant was nearly bankrupt, routinely dismissed by experts as unimaginative, and in sore need of reinvention. Louis V. Gerstner Jr.'s job as the new CEO was to make the company more imaginative and reinvent the business.

His bold move to cut a billion dollars from the research and development budget shocked everybody. "How long before the superiority of our nation is in danger?" asked one of IBM's most respected physicists. "Gerstner is nothing but a cookie seller who has no business tinkering with a technological treasure."

But the billion-dollar cut was anything but self-defeating tinkering. Many of the research scientists were energized. They cleaned out the cobwebs and refocused their thinking, many spending quality time with customers. The result was scores of innovations that matter. Frugal was a catalyst, not a catastrophe.

There are three big reasons why being frugal helps organizations reinvent:

Frugal Is a "Whack on the Side of the Head"

"We all need a whack on the side of the head on occasion to shake us out of our routine patterns, to force us to rethink our problems, and to stimulate us to ask the questions that lead to the right answers," explains creativity expert Roger von Oech.

The great architect Frank Lloyd Wright echoed that sentiment when he wrote in *The Natural House*, "The human race built most nobly when the limitations were the greatest. . . . Limitations seem to have been the best friend of architecture."

Frugal Makes Us Better Stewards of Other People's Money

The bosses at Boo.com are an extreme example of something Nobel Prize winner Milton Friedman wanted everyone to understand about human nature: *We're not very good when we're spending other people's money.* Friedman created this simple chart:

Whose money?	You	Someone Else
YOURS	*Very Careful*	*Careful*
SOMEONE ELSE'S	*Not so careful*	*Not careful at all*

He made the point that the average person gets a better deal and the most value when he spends his own money on himself. When that same person buys someone else a gift or when he uses his company expense account for himself, other considerations and trade-offs inevitably get in the way of grinding out the best deal and greatest value. The absolute worst results, Friedman observed, come when someone else spends a third person's money.

You've probably seen this at work. Headquarters decides to spend big bucks and everyone ends up paying dearly. Imagine all the pain they'll be going through at News Corporation now that the MySpace acquisition, which cost the company $580 million, has been sold for $35 million, literally pennies on the dollar.

That's really what went wrong at Boo. They carelessly spent other people's money.

Compare Boo with James Archer's start-up company. Just a few years before Malmsten and Leander started pitching investors, Archer pitched his own brainchild, Multi-Chem. But since Archer was almost forty, had just lost his job, had no big-money connections, and was not at all chic, he could find only one investor—himself. He launched his idea with all the money he could scrape together—fifty thousand dollars mortgaged from his personal IRA.

Archer was aiming every bit as high as Boo had. His dream was to radically reinvent the business of energy production by providing innovative services and highly productive solutions for oil field operations. In this dream he could see a high-tech laboratory for analyzing and inventing, a state-of-the-art chemical and supply warehouse, snazzy business offices, and a big staff of skilled experts burning with the same passion for the company's mission that he possessed. But since Archer had just fifty thousand dollars in his piggy bank, he had to pinch pennies, testing chemicals in his garage and using the front seat of his old pickup truck as his office.

Working seven days a week, he tackled the problems of clients. He discovered new answers, such as a process to de-liquefy gas wells that increased production, impressing the biggest and the best oil field professionals, including Exxon. As he had no deep pockets to fund a slick promotional campaign, Archer relied on word of mouth to help his business grow. It worked. One by one new customers became loyal users and then told others. Soon he had the money to hire a small staff and rent some space for a warehouse and offices.

And Archer's frugal model keeps working. With the motto "If we don't have it, we'll invent it" and a commitment to "helping the customers profit first," today Multi-Chem has ninety-two locations in the world and is set to hit seven hundred million dollars in sales in the next couple of years.

Frugal Builds Teamwork

There's nothing like being on a winning team to keep a smile on people's faces and build a very collegial environment in which everyone is engaged and on the same page.

As you read in the story at the start of the chapter, not having enough money brought everyone together at Southwest. Twelve different job functions, from flight crews to baggage handlers, all put aside status concerns, job descriptions, and work rules to become a team with a big objective: the ten-minute turn.

With very good reason, another very happy place is the campus of Apple. Last year Apple *grew* its sales by twenty-two billion dollars, which is more than but a handful of companies will ever do in a year. Apple's revenue is now greater than that of Microsoft, the iTunes store does more revenue than the world's biggest music company, and it sells 110,000 iPhones each day. As testament to the passion for change and reinvention that Apple embraces, more than half of the company's revenue comes from products that didn't exist four years ago.

While it would be tempting for a company as spectacularly successful as Apple to be a lavish spender, just the opposite is true. In a typical year it spends $1.7 billion on research and development, compared with Microsoft's nine billion, and it spends one-third of what Microsoft spends on sales and marketing.

You've thought it, I've thought it, every executive and every entrepreneur on the planet has thought it at some point: "If I only had more money, all my problems would disappear."

It's time to realize how wrong we sometimes are. Great companies that embrace radical change and enjoy constant growth find a new path when solving problems and taking advantage of opportunities.

They reject the urge to throw money at their challenges and discipline themselves to do more with less. They practice the Indian path of jugaad and discover there's truth in the adage that all you need to accomplish great things is a problem and not nearly enough money.

GUIDING PRINCIPLES FOR FRUGAL REINVENTION

Make Everything Simple

Einstein wanted fellow scientists to worry about being incomprehensible. "If a physical theory cannot be explained to a child," he told them, "then it's probably worthless." I'd love to say the same thing to everyone who thinks up business strategies.

Arrow Electronics is like all modern businesses: It's a complex business, made more complex by its strategy of taking the customers' thorniest problems on its employees' collective shoulders. So CEO Mike Long and his managers have studied how to make simple sense out of complexity. "The more simple you can make it allows your people to get really focused.

"Back when we were rolling up fifty acquisitions and crossing oceans to grow," says Long, "it would have taken us fourteen pages to explain who we are and where we are going. Now we've learned to make it simple. It doesn't cost you anything—it pays."

Don't let anyone make your business proposition too complicated. If it's already complicated, keep simplifying it until you can explain it to a child without his or her eyes glazing over.

Edit Every "To Do" List

According to the Hackett Group, a global strategic consulting company, the average business tries to manage 372 different objectives during the year. Chances are good that number doesn't surprise you, because you probably live with nearly as many on your plate.

However, Hackett found that leaders at "above average" companies are surprisingly different in this critical measure. They identify an average of just twenty-one priorities instead of 372. Editing the list isn't easy, but the payoff is huge. Time and money get tightly focused on the crucial activities that drive the firm's competitive advantage, and everyone has a clearer idea what to do and no problem deciding who's accountable.

One question I ask each of the thousand CEOs, business owners, entrepreneurs, and senior leaders I speak with each year in preparation for speeches and teaching is, "What's keeping you awake at night, and what are the potential stumbling blocks that might get in the way of your business achieving its full potential?" There are some common answers I frequently hear, but one that's mentioned in almost every conversation is "staying focused," and almost all of them add, "There are so many damn initiatives, plans, programs, decrees, and grand announcements around this place that it's almost impossible to get anything done."

Long believes that "people come to work *wanting* to do their best because that creates enjoyment and fulfillment—they feel like they are making a difference."

So he asked himself a killer question: "What makes the difference between a good hire and a bad one?" The answer, he concluded, is one that's eluded many managers. "A good person knows what they're supposed to do and a bad one isn't sure. I believe the difference between doing a good job and a bad job is clarity . . . and clarity is leadership's responsibility."

Celebrate Frugal Reinvention

In a stony terrain in the south of Sweden, the people of Småland have their own special expression for the art of frugal reinvention, the previously mentioned *lista*, a phrase derived from the Swedish word for "cunning" or "craftiness."

Lista is at the heart of IKEA's incredible success. Leaders at IKEA are determined to avoid spending unless it is really necessary. "If I lower the shelf half a meter, I can make do with my old hand-operated pallet truck. It'll save me having to buy a forklift," they reason. You can find stories of lista in every design and leadership decision at IKEA.

Lista was also at the heart of an incredible, first-of-its-kind accomplishment in IKEA's history. It's the story of "nine in eight," in which IKEA North America got nine new stores designed, engineered, and up and running in just eight short months. Never in IKEA's history had any team accomplished this complex chore so fast.

Most astonishingly of all, the team accomplished this feat frugally, using nothing but existing in-house infrastructure and resources—no additional consulting engineers, no new project coordinators, no logistical outsourcers, and zero additional bureaucracy.

That means a staff of people who had never added more than a store every few years (it took twenty-five years to open nine stores in Canada) charged themselves with planning, building, and merchandising over three million square feet of new retail construction, hiring thirty-three hundred new associates and managers, and purchasing a hundred million dollars of the right new inventory. Like all good stories, this one has a happy ending. "Nine in eight" was a phenomenal success—lista at its very best!

Every company has stories like this, in which employees faced a huge task and meager resources. You read James Archer's story of working magic in his garage laboratory, inventing a process that stunned the deep-pocket researchers at Exxon and made his start-up a world leader. What story can you tell?

Ask WTGBRFSTM: What's the Good Business Reason for Spending This Money?

One of the best frugal reinventors, Mel Haught, of Pella Corporation, teaches us to love dumb questions—good dumb questions such as "Why do we do it that way?" that really clear away the hidden assumptions.

But the best dumb question ever is one I learned from two other frugal reinventors, Herb and Marion Sandler. The Sandlers built one of the most productive and innovative financial institutions by asking themselves and their managers over and over, "What's the good business reason for spending this money?"

That question made the Sandlers' company, World Savings,* an icon of productivity. The business ran with half the staff of its nearest competitor, with each employee generating 40 percent more revenue

---

* I first researched and wrote about World Savings in my 2002 book *Less Is More*. Based on research, I believed then and maintain now that the company was one of the best led and managed businesses that ever existed in the U.S. When they reached their midseventies the Sandlers sold their company to Wachovia, a firm later acquired by Wells Fargo during the real estate meltdown of 2007–2008. Some people in the media attempted to vilify the Sandlers as being part of the real estate meltdown. I believe their forty-two years of stewardship and growth proves otherwise and makes the company they built worthy of study by any serious student of business.

than the industry average of $762,000 per associate, and it delivered double the average profit per employee. By doggedly asking WTG-BRFSTM and demanding a good answer before making any expenditure, the Sandlers and their team achieved 20 percent average compound growth each year for thirty-five consecutive years.

When you examine all you've seen and lived through in business, the magic of asking WTGBRFSTM becomes very clear. How many times have you seen expenditures rationalized because "we did it last year"?

Or how many expenditures have you seen made to put out some fire or respond to what the competition is doing? "When everyone was offering free checking," Marion Sandler recalls, "we considered the costs and asked, 'What's the good business reason for doing this?' and the only way it seemed to work was by feeing the customer to death." That led the leadership to their strategy for attracting new checking customers. "We offered a significant bump [five percent instead of half a percent] in the interest we paid on high balances," she recalls. "It was like someone opened the floodgates!"

Marion pointedly told me in response to my questions about her notorious frugality, "Instead of being surprised at how much we do with so little, I'd honestly like to know how other banks manage to spend so much." I suspect it's because they're afraid to ask WTG-BRFSTM.

Blow Up Any Bureaucracy

An Englishman named Cyril Parkinson analyzed the British Admiralty in 1955 by charting the number of headquarters administrators versus the number of people commanding and running ships and shipyards of the Royal Navy year by year for a decade and a half. Then he saw a surprising pattern in the results. As the number of front-line people doing the actual work decreased 31 percent head-quarters grew 78 percent. This caused Parkinson to produce a mathematical formula that showed that the most natural action of any official was to breed junior officials. Those junior officials would quickly beget their own subordinates, and so it would continue. The work of one would quickly become too much work for seven.

The incentive for each layer in a bureaucracy was that as any subordinate base grew the lead bureaucrat would be promoted. Parkinson had discovered a people pyramid scheme. He called his conclusion the law of the bureaucracy: "Work expands so as to fill the time available."

Five decades and trillions of wasted dollars later, nobody thinks bureaucracy of any kind is funny.

A.T. Kearney research shows that the best performing companies had five hundred fewer managers per billion dollars in sales than poorer performing organizations. It's not hard to see why that happens.

Years back, executives at U.S. Steel saw the threat from Ken Iverson's newly formed Nucor. Innovators inside the executive group drew up plans for a cheap and cheerful mini-mill of their own to compete. But senior financial officers crunched the numbers and scolded them. "It's cheaper to produce more steel from our existing furnaces. Capital costs are covered and all that remains is the variable costs of each extra ton, so it's lots more profitable to continue producing steel the way we do." Technically correct but shortsighted!

FOREVER FRUGAL: ACTION PLAN

▶ Make asking the question "What's the good business reason for spending this money?" part of your culture.

▶ Celebrate wins that embrace the spirit of jugaad, lista, and old-fashioned Yankee ingenuity.

▶ When confronted with a problem or opportunity, gather your key people and brainstorm how to solve the problem or take advantage of the opportunity without using financial resources. You won't always be able to do it, but in many cases you'll end up with a better plan than simply throwing money at something.

▶ Allow your entrepreneurs to be true entrepreneurs; don't kill the dream.

▶ Make yours a culture of problem solving by regularly acknowledging, celebrating, and generously rewarding those who advance your business by identifying the complex problems driving your customers crazy that you can solve.

▶ Consider a pricing model that starts by asking the question "What will the customer pay us for this?" and working backward, instead of taking the position that "this is what it costs us to do it and we'll add our desired margin on top, and that's what customers will have to pay."

▶ Be relentless about simplifying everything without exception.

CHAPTER 8

SYSTEMATIZE
EVERYTHING

"You don't reinvent yourself with as much intentionality as maybe one would think. Sometimes you just look back and say, 'Damn, I reinvented myself.'"

—Pat Lancaster, chairman, Lantech

If the ability to function while holding two opposing ideas in your mind at the same time is the test of high intelligence, then embracing change and reinvention is the ultimate measure of business IQ. Here's the list of opposing ideas that successful reinventors say you need in your head:

- Hold on tight and freely let go.

- Be hard-nosed and soft hearted.

- Focus on a clear destination and search for new horizons.

- Take big risks and make small bets.

- Be frugal and still splurge.

- Think big and act small.

- Be highly creative and obsessively down-to-earth.

- Thoughtfully work your plan and improvise without thinking too much.

Can't you almost hear the naysayers whining, "Would you *puhleese* just make up your mind and pick one or the other?"

We're about to test the limits of your reinvention IQ by asking you to wrap your head around the two polar opposite mind-sets of successful reinventors—the two thoughts they're able to keep in their heads, and that you need to keep in yours; the yin and the yang of constant reinventing: Leading change means systematizing everything.

One of the findings for my 2001 book *Less Is More* was that the most productive companies in the world routinely systematized everything. The research for this book turned up the same finding: Companies that do the best job of embracing constant change, growth, and reinvention make it look easy, because they've systematized and scaled all the core business practices.

Systematizing means determining the best way to do something (step-by-step), making certain everyone does his or her part the same way (without significant variation), and then using the system as a baseline for continual improvement.

Many people hate the thought of the functions they perform being systematized. Almost universally they complain that it will stifle their imagination, destroy their creativity, and take away their freedom. These are all weak excuses for the two real reasons they don't want any part of a systematized process: They're either too inflexible to learn a new way of doing things or they're scared to death of the accountability that systematization will bring.

Before answering all the objections people have about the S-word, I want to tell you a story about a woman who emigrated from Germany to the United States, who held those two opposing thoughts—leading change and systematizing everything—in her head and built a business that she sold for three-quarters of a billion dollars.

"I was a toddler when my father died, just a month before World

War Two ended," Christel DeHaan recounts. "Our life in postwar Germany was very, very, very difficult." The family lived in a small four-hundred-year-old stone house in a walled village that had been founded in the middle ages. Christel carried water home from a nearby creek, stocked the basement with coal and the attic with apples. Meat was so scarce and unaffordable that her mother, Anna, at times turned to a horse butcher.

"I wouldn't trade my upbringing for anything," says DeHaan. "My mother had very high expectations for my sister and me to be honorable human beings and be very persistent, hardworking, and to never give up. I was very fortunate. She inspired me and gave me a love for my life."

DeHaan went to England as a nanny after high school and then got hired by the U.S. Army because of her language skills. She married a man from Indiana and they lived in Indianapolis. While her marriage did not last, she was again very fortunate. "I met Jon DeHaan and fell in love with him and later his great idea for a new business," she says.

Jon was intrigued by a new idea that allowed motor-home owners to exchange the pads they purchased in RV parks with owners from other parks all over America. For example, if one bought a space for his Winnebago near Yosemite he could trade it for a week near Disneyland.

Jon reasoned that if someone created a similar reciprocal system for vacation condominium owners, it would help the developers and builders of recreational resorts sell more units by adding a unique selling feature: the ability to trade weeks with other owners in other desirable locations.

For example, you might own a vacation condominium in the Finger Lakes region of New York and exchange a week or two to stay at another owner's condominium near Disneyland. No one would have to buy another place or rent hotel rooms in all the destinations they wanted to visit. They could buy one unit and a low-cost annual membership in RCI (Resort Condominiums International) and exchange weeks with other owners in other locations.

In order to make it work, the DeHaans would first have to convince resort owners that an exchange would make them more successful. At the same time, the systems would have to fairly value each condominium, realizing that times of the year are not all equal, unit sizes and amenities come in every possible configuration, and what customers desire keeps changing. It would take an equation worthy of a rocket scientist to tame all the variables.

"How do you cope with all that and put it into in a tight-functioning system that everyone could trust and find satisfactory?" Christel asks. She was steadfast in her core belief that "you have to be honest and your word must be honored."

The answer was to marry the detail oriented with the creative, the outgoing marketer with the inside analyst, the visionary with the process engineer: Jon and Christel.

Proving again that great companies are seldom born of unlimited resources, the frugal first headquarters of RCI was an antique roll-top desk in the DeHaans' Indianapolis living room. Christel did it all through the U.S. Postal Service, keeping track on index cards organized in shoe boxes and obsessing over creating a tight, well-functioning system that was fair, accurate, consistent, and predictable. Trust was paramount, and any action that would cause distrust was her foe.

"At the end of our first year we had about twenty resorts that had signed up," says the extraordinarily well-spoken Christel. "I spent all my time on building and systematizing the exchange structure."

But the sheer complexity of a fair exchange was greater than the best minds and manual systems. Thank God it was 1977 and the desktop computer had recently been invented. Christel re-created her manual system on a Wang system and Wang software and then reinvented it again for the IBM platform. It's important to remember that in those days "user friendly" was still decades away. Converting manual systems to software code took tedious hours of painstaking effort—reading technical manuals, writing equations, inputting data, and debugging all the spreadsheets.

But Christel (and by extension the business) was fortunate. She had a great head on her shoulders. Not only could she work her way through the unfriendly software to craft a solution; persist until her process was fair, accurate, consistent, and trustworthy; and take apart the system every two years and reengineer it for bigger, better, faster computers in a business that began growing geometrically from its first-year revenues of fourteen thousand dollars; but still she could show respect and deep admiration for the entrepreneurial, marketing, emotional, chaotic, innovative *other* side of the business.

This is rare. Every office and cubicle in business runs with blinders on, seeing their specialty as very important and underappreciated, while underappreciating all the others. Sales gets snarky about accounting, accountants roll their eyes at flamboyant sales types, front-line managers and HR can't stand each other, and the boss . . . well, he's the reason *The Office* is a worldwide hit for Ricky Gervais and Stephen Merchant.

Says Christel: "I so admired Jon DeHaan for the yeoman's work of landing the developers and handling the outside. I think that's what set us apart [from the copycats who followed RCI's lead]. Other companies push the visionary and business-development goals, while the operating side doesn't deliver what's been promised. I believed commitments must be honored and the consumer must be protected. So we invested in both sides and created our systems with the same tenacity and the same sense of urgency, with the same spirit of innovation as we sold ourselves."

Shortly after forming RCI, which allowed condominium owners to exchange weeks with other owners, the DeHaans were the beneficiaries of some very good luck, if you agree that the best definition of *luck* is when preparedness meets opportunity.

Timeshares were beginning to really take off, and the DeHaans realized that they represented a potential gold mine for the company. A standard timeshare allows a customer to buy as little as one week or as many weeks as he or she wishes in a resort property. The weeks belong to the buyer forever. Buying a timeshare locks in and prepays someone's vacation perpetually, but the downside is that with a traditional timeshare you have to go back to the same destination every year.

The DeHaans quickly determined that if a timeshare developer were able to offer an annual membership in RCI, which would allow people who purchased timeshare weeks to exchange them for weeks at other properties, there'd be no stopping them and that it would provide a valuable sales tool for the developers of timeshare properties.

"It simply took off," says Christel. "In the first decade we doubled our revenues every year. Good economy or bad, recession or recovery, real estate market up or down, it didn't matter; it just kept growing and never dropped."

Jon and Christel eventually divorced in the late 1980s, in a courtroom struggle that lasted eighteen months, during which Jon claimed he was entitled to 80 percent of the company and Christel only 20 percent. The judge ultimately ruled that the couple should split the company fifty-fifty, and because Christel was willing to pay more for Jon's half than he for hers, she quickly arranged to borrow eighty million dollars and bought his half in 1989. By then, thanks to her love of learning and a mind that was incessantly systematizing everything, she was ready for the challenge. The business continued to grow fast, and just nine short years after buying Jon out, Christel and her team made the company worth ten times what she'd paid Jon.

"Over the years I'd had many offers to sell the company," she says. "People were knocking on the door all the time wanting to buy the company, but I just wasn't ready yet. I wanted to climb even steeper mountains and help lead the company to new destinations." In 1996 Christel got a call from Henry Silverman, a Wall Street entrepreneur best known for cobbling together the various travel reservation services, hotels, car rental companies, and real estate brokerage companies that eventually became Cendant Corporation, and she said to herself, "Maybe it's time to listen."

"My mother always told me that it was better to leave a party five minutes early rather than one minute too late, and I realized it was time to leave. The company has lots of oxygen left," Christel says, "and there were all kinds of dynamics with everything else Cendant owned that would allow everyone to prosper." So she took the money and set out on her next *global* reinvention effort, which you'll read about later in this book.

Starting out with index cards stored in a shoe box on a kitchen table, RCI now serves more than four million clients and forty-four hundred resorts and is in more than a hundred countries.

RCI somewhat lost its way and stumbled a bit after Christel DeHaan left. Instead of balancing the two opposing ideas of constant change and systems for everything, the new managers were mesmerized by the latest fad that they were sure was going to deliver a big score, or a new pot of gold to chase, or the brilliant idea that was going to be the next killer app. Of course, that didn't happen.

Enter new CEO Geoff Ballotti. Ballotti, who at age twenty-seven was already a top gun at Bank of New England (with a five-hundred-million-dollar loan portfolio) and then became a Six Sigma executive at Starwood Hotels & Resorts, had been a fan of RCI for more than a decade. "It was one of the most innovative business ideas I'd ever seen," Ballotti says. "But it was the culture that attracted me the most. DeHaan had created a culture that was continually innovating, and everyone was always looking at the horizon, where it wasn't just about this year but the next year and the year after that. I loved that her whole team had embraced her style of being disciplined, organized, methodical, and systematic. I was psyched to join the team."

Ballotti also saw the error of the previous manager's ways. "We saw that as the credit markets dried up and real estate got tight, developers would stop building at the double-digit pace that had fueled our growth. We had to figure out a way to come up with big innovations, embrace change, and invent new services and products that would differentiate us from our competition and would let us grow faster than our industry. We were waiting for big ideas instead of using a system to innovate."

Ballotti also took a hard look inside the organization. "The team was exceptional," he explains, "but millions of our members were frustrated with us. Our search wasn't great, our Web site wasn't great, and our 'sold out' messages were infuriating clients."

The new CEO went to work like a black belt—disciplined, persistent, aggressive, focused, and systematic. First he launched a radical reinvention of RCI's currency that allowed the company to do far more than facilitate trading weeks. "Gordon [Gurnick, RCI's president] had this idea and it was brilliant," says Ballotti. "He created a system where every day, every timeshare at every resort owned by every member is valued in increments called RCI Points.

"It was one of the most complex mind benders, requiring an army of so-smart-they're-scary Ph.D.s using revenue-management formulas and supercomputers. Their algorithms ran every night, valuing each piece of the puzzle," he says. "It was like creating the New York Stock Exchange for vacation time, which allowed people with Starwood, Hilton, Hyatt, Marriott, or Disney Club membership to enjoy four thousand additional resorts all over the world, plus hotel stays, airplane tickets, golf outings, five-star dinners—everything. This innovation attracted new developers, made our members even happier, and delivered more revenues, business, and earnings."

Next, Ballotti turned the search function upside down. "Members might want Waikiki Beach at Christmas but own Branson, Missouri, during the rainiest time of the year. Well, there's no way they'd have the currency for that exchange. When they'd try to do an exchange the system would come back saying 'sold out' and 'unavailable.' People would get mad because the salesman sold them the idea that the exchange would put them in Paris or Disney World. And the member would be mad at us instead of the salesperson who'd promised the moon for peanuts.

"So we asked, 'What if all our members deposited the time they own and rather than tell us where and when they'd like to go, we gave them a list of all the places they could go?' " Ballotti continues. "We've got millions of options at any one time, so we could give them thousands of choices and a chance to drill down to their heart's desire. So instead of getting a 'sold out' message they get choices like Maine or Cape Cod." This reinvention improved member satisfaction and increased online transactions 500 percent.

Now, as Ballotti has the next big reinvention under way, he's still guided by the head and heart of Christel DeHaan: "To wake up every day with one objective in mind, to make our four million members and the owners of our forty-four hundred affiliated resorts happy they've chosen us to make their dreams come true."

LESSONS FROM RCI

Appreciate All Sides of the Business

Christel DeHaan, motivated by the twin guiding principles of organization and never disappointing a customer, realized that the company's customer service experience had to be fair, transparent, reliable, and completely systematized. Still, like in a good marriage, she maintained a heartfelt appreciation for the other side (the entrepreneurial, constantly seeking change side) of the business.

Appreciation is another of the soft skills that consistently drive the hard results we all want to achieve. When I studied how the *Wall Street Journal* was able to get everyone to buy in and follow through on a disruptive but necessary strategic initiative, the executive who led the charge, Joanne Lipman, was clearly more successful because of her extraordinary capacity to appreciate. In fact, she used the word *love* more often than I'd ever heard in any business interview. For example, when I asked if all the egos and turf battles frustrated her, she replied, "I love consensus kinds of projects. There are a ton of smart people here, and I love hearing what they have to say."

When I asked how she kept everyone motivated and accountable over the many months and through countless unanticipated obstacles (including senior staff who outranked her and board members who had priorities outside the *WSJ*), she explained, "After I nagged them, I made sure to shower them with love."

This executive told me she *loved* the fact that everyone had their own, often different ideas and insisted on "being heard." She *loved* fitting all the pieces, personalities, and priorities together. She even *loved* giving others all the credit, making sure everyone saw their fingerprints on the project's success.

It was a bit hard to believe. I thought she might be winding me up. So I asked the highly experienced outside change consultant who had observed her firsthand throughout the many months of the initiative. I knew he'd be a credible source. "People really responded to her," he confirmed. "She got more cooperation and a greater willingness to pitch in and solve problems. It was amazing."

I learned a big lesson from her: Don't underappreciate the power of appreciation.

Systems Allow for Successful Scaling

Every entrepreneur thinks about how his or her idea will be scaled, or grown big enough and quickly enough to create a real competitive advantage. But scale can't happen until there are systems.

If Christel DeHaan hadn't systematized the use of index cards describing each condominium filed in her shoe boxes, RCI would not have been able to grow double digits each year for decades.

To scale any business you must first create a reliable system for all functions—manufacturing, sales, promotion, talent acquisition, innovation, even leadership from the CEO. "In our industry," Mike Long says emphatically, "if you say you can do something, you'd *better well do it*. Our path to doubling our sales to forty billion dollars means scaling at the same pace as we chase the sales."

Systems Allow You to Solve Problems and Take Advantage of New Opportunities Faster

People imagine that systems will bog you down. But repeatable and reliable systems actually make a business more nimble. RCI was able to quickly capitalize on the boom in timeshare sales, which began just a year after their company was founded, because Christel DeHaan hadn't waited to develop systems and was able to quickly move her system from index cards to Wang computers and then to IBM PCs in order to create a more reliable exchange process for all her clients.

"In 2008," Pat Lancaster, of packaging industry leader Lantech, reveals, "our phones stopped ringing for *sixty days*. New orders slowed to panic levels, and our business went to half our run rate overnight. What saved us was the speed with which we shifted our resources and focus. We made changes that would normally be resisted."

Lancaster credits his decade and a half of systematizing everything from the manufacturing floor to the CEO's office, along with three rounds of reinvention, for making everyone nimble and less resistant to trying new routines. "We never had a month we didn't make a profit through that entire period. Production people were shifted from the shop floor into uncharted territory—systematizing the D in our R and D and bringing a long list of new concepts to our customers quicker. Now our future is even brighter."

He's confident systematizing will continue to make Lantech fast. Around the world, about three billion pallet loads a year are shipped using Lantech's processes and equipment. "We don't touch them all," Lancaster says, "yet!"

Good Systems Generate Great Customer Service Experiences

When Geoff Ballotti became CEO of RCI, the company had loads of unhappy customers, because salespeople for timeshare developers had led buyers to believe they could exchange a week in Biloxi for a week in New York and many of those customers were receiving scores of "sold out" or "not available" messages during their searches.

So RCI created a system that gave customers an extensive list of what they *could* have instead of what they didn't qualify for, and its online business and customer satisfaction soared. (Imagine the goodwill that could be generated by any airline brave enough to do the same for members of its mileage programs.)

"Gartner research says that thirty-eight percent of travel revenue is booked online. We're now approaching seventy percent . . . because we're so manic about making that search experience easy as it can be," Ballotti says. "And now we're just completing a new system, three years in development, using even more complex algorithms, to value each unit of inventory that projects value six months in advance, so members can get their best exchange plans and satisfy their heart's desire. These new systems will positively delight our members and create big opportunities for our developers."

THE S-WORD

When I first created the outline for this chapter my working title was "Systematize Everything (That Can Be Systematized)." I wanted to avoid controversy with the many executives who insist that systematizing *their* area would choke off their chances for success. For example, Eric Schmidt, former CEO of Google, was adamant in explaining why innovation could *not* be systematized: "Measuring it would choke it off altogether."

But then I remembered what A. G. Lafley, CEO at highly innovative Procter & Gamble, said about innovation. "It is possible to measure the yield of each process, the quality, and the end result." Lafley quickly brought systematization to the innovation process at P&G, creating the Living It program, putting employees in the homes of customers to systematically observe their challenges and processes; Working It, to connect company decision makers with the front lines of their channel partners; and Connect and Develop, to combat the insular, not-invented-here blinders and realize that lots of innovation happens outside Procter & Gamble's walls.

Pat Lancaster is characteristically blunt: "There's absolutely *no* good reason systematizing isn't valuable in every part of the business."

Lantech's latest systematizing has dared to measure and improve the last "don't go there" sacred cow in all organizations—the CEO function. "In most companies of any size," he explains, "leadership doesn't have a clue about what's really going on at *the ground floor*. Sure, they have these eleventh-floor strategic imperatives with grandiose controls, but they don't really connect and don't really address the problems.

"So we systematized the CEO's day, starting at eight forty-five a.m. He leaves the office and begins with a walk-around [not the traditional MBWA—management by walking around—you read about in books and magazines]. He makes a purposeful, systematic visit in person to thirteen core result centers with a daily agenda to review the work for the day, the problems and the speed bumps of the day. Moving in this loop day in and out, he gets a much better understanding, gets to help flatten any speed bumps, review the solutions from his leadership and keep everyone accountable. I know it sounds very tedious and un-CEO-like, but the nimbleness of finding and resolving problems quickly has made for huge improvements in our business. In a market that's still thirty percent off its pre-2008 revenue rates, we're back to level and slightly up."

Seeing how Lafley has systematized innovation and the team at Lantech has systematized top leadership, there's no reason to suggest any function is off-limits. You just need to systematize your approach.

I told you earlier that there are two honest reasons so many people hate the thought of the functions they perform being systematized:

Either they're too inflexible to learn a new way of doing things, or they're scared to death of the accountability that systematization will bring.

I'd like to amend that list with a third reason some legitimately hate the S-word: The systematization was botched by poor execution by a previous boss or at some previous company. I've spent twenty years doing postmortems on botched systematization attempts and kept a list of the don'ts. Here are the top five.

Don't Let Systematization Become an Excuse for Getting Rule Bound

Rule bound is a phrase I got from IDEO general manager Tom Kelley. It means having unnecessary procedures and bureaucratic rules that adversely affect morale and personal creativity.

"I have a friend," Kelley says by way of example. "She went to work for a law firm. Her second day she pinned up a poster, a nice poster, really a piece of art in her personal work space. Within an hour someone from HR came and took it down. My friend was informed *she had broken the rules of the office.* 'First of all, *we* do not use pushpins here,' the HR manager said with one of those forced, bureaucratic smiles, 'and second, any personal art must first be approved by the art committee.'"

That example reminded me of another incident at a big successful media company.

"What happened to my chair?" Leslie asked the person in the next cubicle. Her ergonomic chair with arms had been replaced by an armless version. "I don't know," he said, "But mine's gone too." Being seven months pregnant, Leslie needed the arms to get up from her desk without losing her balance. So the next morning the mom-to-be went to an empty office and retrieved a chair with arms. That night the chairs were switched again. So the next morning Leslie swapped chairs again. That evening the chairs were switched yet again, but this time with a memo pinned to the seat: "The new furniture policy is that all cubicles in your group are to have desk chairs *without arms*."

Think about it. By removing the poster and switching the chairs and then scolding both women as if they were misbehaving children, each company sent a terrible signal: We don't respect you; we suspect you; we're watching you.

No wonder people hate the idea of systems. Uptight administrators with issues turn process into an excuse for a process police state.

Don't Go with Anything but the BEST Idea

Pat Lancaster came up with his ingenious idea for shrink-wrapping pallets of materials and cumbersome batches of boxes thirty-five years ago. He patented the idea—and many subsequent iterations— and built Lantech, a company that became a world leader in manufacturing large and expensive shrink-wrapping machines. Business boomed, and Lancaster admits, "We probably became a little complacent and generally acted more out of our interests than the customers'. It was a simple proposition," he says. "We had the patent on the best way to shrink-wrap whatever needed wrapping, and if someone wanted one they bought it from us on our terms."

Eventually the company's patents expired, other companies began copying their designs, and suddenly they had low-cost competition. Battles raged all the way to the Supreme Court as Lantech's principals tried to protect what they saw as rightfully theirs, but Lancaster says that on the day the courts ruled against them, he knew the game had changed.

"I knew that modest improvements in manufacturing, sales, and customer service wouldn't be sufficient and that radical changes had to be made fast," he says.

Lancaster hired Anand Sharma, CEO of TBM Consulting Group and a man named by *Fortune* magazine as one of America's Heroes of Manufacturing, to assist the company in a dramatic and swift turnaround.

They shut down the assembly line one weekend, turned off the IBM material planning system the company had invested millions of dollars in, and said, "We're never going back to doing things the way we did, and within five days we have to have a new way of doing things."

With Sharma's guidance the forty team members selected for the reinvention mapped the firm's current processes, collectively designed new ones, and set a series of objectives. Two days into the five-day exercise Sharma, a native of India and someone intimately familiar with the principles of jugaad, anxiously waited for the question that's generally asked by a team member on the second day of one of his interventions.

"Eventually someone raises their hand and asks, 'When are we going to begin actually doing what we're talking about?' "

Sharma's answer is always the same: "Let's do it right now!" Then he gives them the process.

"We're going to break into work units, clean and scrub an area of the factory floor, and begin building," he says. "And we're not going to spend any money making the changes. If something doesn't work we'll fix it. We want creativity before capital and quick and crude rather than slow and elegant."

Lancaster remembers, "It was an exhilarating experience, one of the best in my life." Over two days the forty team members constructed a new temporary facility out of cardboard, wood, whatever was required, and began manufacturing.

Lancaster says that the magic around a reinvention intervention is that the people involved in the process have a say but the establishment—the leadership—doesn't. "I was there as one member of a team wearing jeans and working alongside everyone else," says Lancaster, "not as a boss, owner, or CEO."

The team Lancaster was on was tasked with coming up with a temporary turntable out of wood that would be essential in the new manufacturing process. Lancaster says he had an idea how it should look and convinced the team to do it his way. "We finished at ten that night," he says, "and we couldn't wait to show the entire team our *too cool* new design."

What Lancaster's team didn't know was that another team was also working on the same turntable, and when they were both presented to the group it was obvious the other team's was far superior to his.

"To this day," he says, "the entire company talks about the night they put the boss's design in the Dumpster."

The results of Lantech's reinvention were dramatic. For years the company had routinely increased productivity 1 percent per month; after the reinvention it grew sales 300 percent without adding a single person to the head count, and it slashed the production time for manufacturing its products from five weeks to just eleven hours (an astonishing 98 percent reduction).

What occurred with Lancaster's turntable idea during Lantech's reinvention intervention answers one of the most fundamental questions about embracing change: Whose idea wins? The answer, of course, is that the best idea should win—not the boss's idea, not the boss's kid's idea, not the strategy department's idea, not the old idea, not the competition's idea; only the *best* idea should win.

Don't Rely on Anyone's Memory for Systems Decisions—Use Data

One of my favorite CEOs reminds me often that "memories are convenient." What he means is we more readily remember events that prove we're right. It's a disease that adversely affects our decisions and our ability to learn new things. And the only cure is the bitterest pill of all to swallow: We have to keep track and use the data, instead of our memories, for decisions.

During a flight a few years ago I had a conversation with the national sales manager of a large drug company about systems. His position was that he hated being forced to do things a certain way and therefore had hated systems as a salesman, and as sales manager he didn't want systematization.

My position was that every function—in which you can determine a best way to do something and make certain that it's done that way by everyone without variation and is then constantly improved—could and should be systematized. That included sales.

"There is no best way to sell," he said. "You just hire good people and let them do their thing, as long as they don't break any laws."

The data says otherwise. Researchers examined the performance of sales executives such as those in his industry to discover if there was indeed a best way to sell. Fifteen thousand critical data points were analyzed, and when they compared the most effective one-third of the sales professionals to the less effective two-thirds, researchers found seven specific competencies—seven activities or behaviors—that separated the best from the rest. These successful practices did not vary across industries; they are universal. Most important, the seven competencies can be taught, measured, and therefore systematized.

Footnote to that study: When sales managers and VPs were asked to list the critical skills that would predict better performance in sales, they chose factors that didn't make the list of the top seven. I'll bet that when each was asked why he or she chose those factors, they all used their memories to recount a story that justified their thinking.

As for that VP of sales sharing my row on that flight, a quick data search following our original conversation revealed that ten thousand dollars invested in his company five years earlier was worth sixty-two hundred, versus a sector performance of $18,500. I checked again recently and learned that his company no longer exists. After the company paid record fines totaling hundreds of millions of dollars for illegal bribes and payoffs made by him and his salespeople, the remnants got sopped up by another company.

Don't Create Mean Systems

Facing tough competition, unrelenting demands for greater productivity, and intense time pressures, and navigating market conditions that are as turbulent as Colorado River white water, many executives feel they have to take extreme action. "We are going to be lean and mean," they'll announce.

I agree. As I wrote in *Less is More*, lean systems are an absolute business necessity. But it bears repeating that meanness adds no value whatsoever to lean systems. All mean systems do is keep leaders from discovering problems before they blow up into disasters, unleash a lot of bad judgments and ethical lapses, and cost you money.

Important and valuable systems of accountability are particularly vulnerable to being mean. Take the case of Richard Brown, at Electronic Data Systems (EDS), for example.

Brown took the reins in 1999. He was handed a company mired in quarter after quarter of no growth and declining earnings. He studied the causes and determined rightly that internal, controllable issues were at the root of the shortfall. He decided EDS needed to change internally, reinvent itself, and become much more accountable.

Next, Brown set top-down goals that he considered a stretch (others saw them as impossible) and created a system to hold his leadership's feet to the performance fire.

The accountability system instituted a monthly conference call with 150 executives on the line, in which the CEO grilled anyone who missed their targets with harsh questioning. "He'd ask you *why* in front of everyone," a former manager told the *Wall Street Journal*. But he didn't really want to hear why. What the CEO expected was that the underperforming manager would explain on the spot what was going to be done to get back on plan.

Brown made it clear that poor performers would shape up or leave. And when an executive piped up and said he was worried about the anxiety and stress in his operating unit, Brown's response was blistering. "This is a test of leadership," he said. "You show me an organization that's wringing its hands, listening to rumors, anxious about their future . . . and I will show you leadership that behaves the same way. I can't believe this worry is fact based. I believe this worry is ignorance based. And if that's the case, it's your fault."

The fear-of-God stuff worked for a while. Nearly eighty-nine million dollars in new contracts came in, and EDS had eleven quarters of double-digit growth in operating margins and earnings per share. But as a giant in the early days of leadership science counseled her students, "The highest-grade thinking does not merely address the present. . . . It is the leftover in any decision where you find its real value."

Here are the leftovers from his decision. Fifteen months later several of EDS's new mega-clients fell into bankruptcy, leaving huge liabilities, while many others had their contracts renegotiated down; cash flow dropped; the company was slapped with fines in settling

SEC charges for accounting irregularities; earnings warnings were issued; the stock tanked; and Brown was asked for his resignation.

These are the all-too-predictable outcomes of a mean accountability system that forced upper managers to say "I screwed up" in front of 150 peers, ridiculed their concerns and labeled them "hand wringing" and "ignorant," and fired people for not delivering on top-down goals. Why would anyone expect anything but cover-ups and ethical lapses?

Mean systems scapegoat and demoralize. They attack people instead of problems. They're a relic of a primitive and superstitious past. They are not data driven.

Don't Insist on Going It Alone

"I really like your hypothesis, Jason," Pat Lancaster said in his typical straight-talking, unequivocal way. "But . . ."

I had sent him the opening paragraphs of this chapter, about holding two opposing thoughts in order to reinvent, with the two most opposing of all being change and systematizing. I wanted his feedback, but now I was nervous to hear the other shoe drop. "Yes, Pat," I replied, "but what?"

"But I've never seen those two capabilities embodied in the same person where either one or the other didn't dominate. Take me, for example. During the formative years at Lantech I had to stifle my creative juices in order to make the stability of systems happen. It set up a frustration in me which made things less than perfect.

"Now we have two separate human beings, me and the CEO, and we each embody one of the two sides. Our CEO is a zealot for systems—lean, productive, high-quality systems. He can freeze a dynamic process, plug and unplug every piece, and improve it so that it is more reliable, of higher quality, and incredibly productive. He allows me to now be the rowdy counter-ego that's continually pressuring to do something wild, crazy, and disruptive to the status quo. That produces not a small amount of conflict and friction between the revolutionary view and the hold of the current systems-stable view. But we work it out.

"Now that I'm free to be the alter ego and focus on the pressure points in our customers' operations," Lancaster continues, "I'm figuring out their problems and pain in their processes. I come back from my time on the shop floor at Procter and Gamble, Pepsi, Coke, Kimberly Clark, et cetera, with a vision of the systems and products that could address their concerns . . . many ideas that [the clients] can't even see themselves. And then the two sides of Lantech meet."

Bull's-eye! Lancaster takes us back to where we started, but with a brilliant twist. The test of intelligence is indeed the ability to hold two opposing thoughts in one's mind, appreciate both, and still function. But you don't have to be the be-all and end-all expert in your business at one side or the other. In fact, you can be the one who doesn't excel at either. You can be the one who appreciates both and creates the conditions for both sides to flourish.

Don't try to live the myth that the boss has to be the smartest person in the room and the best at everything to succeed. It's not data driven.

In the next chapter, we'll explore what's holding you back from embracing constant change and reinvention.

SYSTEMATIZE EVERYTHING: ACTION PLAN

▶ As you work with a small team composed of leadership, management, and workers, make a list of every function in your business that can be systematized, from answering the telephone to making sales calls to the final delivery of a product or service. A correct list will include almost every task within the department or company.

▶ Work with your team to prioritize the order for systematizing each task.

▶ With input from the team, the people performing the task or function, and your customers, determine the best practice for each function or task and begin the process of systematization. The end goal of systematization is to deliver what's been promised in the most efficient, productive and cost-effective manner.

▶ Put in place mechanisms designed to constantly improve what's been systematized, with the input of all the partners involved.

▶ Don't underestimate the power of appreciation, and constantly strive to acknowledge people for their contributions; the payoff will be immense.

▶ Systematize each leader's first hour of the day. The first hour should be a purposeful, walk-around-talk-around to and with each core result center, with an agenda to review the workload, possible problems, and speed bumps of the day.

▶ Consciously work to develop an appreciation for the other parts of the business. This one bucks human nature and must become intentional.

CHAPTER 9

DON'T HESITATE

On the plains of hesitation bleach the bones of countless millions who on the dawn of victory paused to rest, and while resting died.

—George W. Cecil, advertisement for
correspondence school, 1928

esitation holds people and companies back from embracing change and reinvention. Until people are able to figure out how to deal with the natural tendency to hesitate and drag their feet because of their fear of the unknown, no meaningful reinvention will occur.

Nobody loves stories about good fortune happening to good people more than I do. Recently I learned the details of three such stories, and each puts a big smile on my face that reappears whenever I think about them. Each story contains a few choice takeaways about dealing with the hesitation that's naturally present in all our lives.

FROM BEANS TO BANKING

My friend Todd Nagel is the president of River Valley Bank, in Wisconsin and Michigan, and he loves telling stories about how his company's original founder enthusiastically embraced radical change and reinvention sixty years ago.

Back in the 1940s, when a huge migration of people in the United

States was heading west to California, Ron Nicklaus's father did the reverse and headed to Wisconsin, where he began a dairy farm with the one cow he could afford to purchase. Nicklaus remembers his father as someone who "would get an idea, set aside any hesitation, take a chance, and work like heck to make it happen."

Ron inherited his dad's reinvention genes, and in the 1950s, when he was twenty years old, he became interested in the fertilization and growth of plants and purchased a truck, trailer, and applicator to fertilize other farmers' fields. He thought he'd be fertilizing corn, but when he realized that most farmers also raised beans, a crop that annoyingly had to be harvested by hand, he hesitated just a bit. Realizing he could help the famers by figuring out a way to harvest their beans with a machine, he thought about buying one of the first mechanical bean harvesters. It would mean changing his initial plans, but there was more opportunity in harvesting beans than fertilizing fields.

Ron knew the importance of scaling his business long before the word became a business buzzword. He put the pedal to the metal and within two years the family enterprise was harvesting beans all over the central U.S. from early spring to late fall.

By the early 1960s, Ron had married his sweetheart and quickly had a baby boy named Todd, followed by Greg a few years later. The family traveled together harvesting beans and organizing the distribution schedule of eighty semitrucks filled with beans. Business was great, but Ron sensed yet another opportunity. This time, he didn't waste a moment hesitating.

The family began manufacturing bean harvesters themselves and quickly started another venture in which they bought raw land, set up the irrigation systems (which were new at the time), and expanded into planting and harvesting their own fields.

By the mid-1970s, Ron had become intrigued with the idea of

owning a bank. "Over the years," he says, "we'd borrowed a lot of money from banks and we'd spent a lot of time teaching banks how to lend to us, and I wanted to own a bank that could truly work with the unique needs and ideas of people."

While Todd and Greg continued running the huge bean-harvesting business, Ron began selling the family's farms in order to finance the purchase of their first bank. In 1983, after looking at more than thirty possible acquisitions, he purchased River Valley Bank, which today has eighteen highly successful locations spanning two states and where the telephone is always answered, "Have an incredible day!"

It's normal to have some hesitation when it comes to business ventures, but Ron's determination to constantly test his limits and achieve better tomorrows for his family always won out as he went from beans to banking.

THE TAXI DRIVER

Last year while staying at our summer home in northern Michigan, I found myself frequently flying out of the small airport on research trips and speeches. Because one of my arrivals was going to be late in the evening and I didn't want family members to make the drive, I called and reserved a taxi to make sure I'd have a ride back to the lake.

As I walked through security I breathed a sigh of relief when I saw a man holding a sign with my name. "Hi, I'm Jared, your driver," the young man said, and we shook hands, got my bags in the car, and began the hour-long drive. I had a few calls to make and a few texts to send and then settled back to enjoy the ride.

The driver had turned down the radio when I was making my calls, so the car was silent for a time. Finally, wanting for some conversation, I said to the driver—keeping in mind that despite it being a tourist area, this is a place where almost everybody knows almost everybody else—"What's your story? How'd you end up here driving a taxi?"

I caught his big grin in the rearview mirror as he responded, "Well, I guess you could say that I'm keeping my hands dirty."

His words stunned me. Those words are mine. I've written about keeping your hands dirty in previous books, and they've been part of every speech I've ever given. The words speak to the need for every business manager and leader to always stay close to customers so they know what's really going on.

He caught my surprise and said, "Caught you off guard, huh? I can quote lots of things from all your books. I'm actually the owner of the company and wanted to meet you, so that's why I'm driving you tonight."

I'm not sure how many taxicab drivers or taxicab company owners have read my books, so I prodded further to learn more about Jared.

Jared grew up on a farm in the upper Midwest, went to college, and began teaching high school history and coaching football in Bakersfield, California, when he came across one of those book-and-video programs sold on television infomercials about striking it rich in real estate. He quickly bought his first few houses and rented them out according to the formula provided. His wife wasn't so gung ho, but he eventually got her on board, and they began buying as many homes as they were able.

A few years later he heard about a townhouse development near his hometown whose developer was in financial trouble, and he figured out that if he cashed out of California he'd have enough to buy the development for four million dollars and they'd be back where they'd always wanted to be. He hesitated a bit. They were building a great life in California, the weather was terrific, and they'd be taking a big chance. But they were young and had figured out how to attain almost 100 percent occupancy of the homes they rented, so they faced their fears head-on and pulled the pin.

Jared, age thirty-one, and his wife and three small children now own nearly one hundred houses, townhouses, and condominiums, and I was curious how being an acquisitive landlord had led him to the taxi business.

"A few years ago," he said, "I was interested in buying a house that was for sale, and when I was going through it I saw an old Checker taxi in the garage and asked about it, and it turned out that the homeowner had tried starting a taxi company, found the sledding too tough, and had given it up, so I bought the house along with the old taxi and restarted the defunct taxi company," he said, adding, "What did I have to lose?

"I got a few cars, hired a few drivers, and did all the dispatching myself," Jared said, "which gave me a unique opportunity of asking everyone who called what other services we could offer them. People started asking us about limos for weddings and VIPs and then small buses for tours, and then I landed a contract with the airport to transport passengers whose flights had been canceled to other airports. Now we have a pretty big fleet of vehicles, and I get to provide employment for lots of good people."

"What's your endgame?" I wanted to know.

"Oh, there's no endgame and there's no destination," he replied. "I'm having more fun than I ever imagined possible, and I just want to keep going, keep discovering other opportunities and having more fun."

We'd long since arrived at the lake and were sitting in the

driveway as Jared shared one more thought, in response to my questioning whether he'd ever found what he does hard and stressful and what advice he'd offer others.

"The most surprising thing," he said, "is how easy it is. My wife and I have built this thing in the middle of the worst economic downturn that's ever hit the U.S. I'm a college graduate and a former teacher but probably don't have superior intellect," he continued, adding, "Anyone can do the same thing if they're willing to get over their hesitation, keep their eyes open to opportunity, work real hard, and make a few small bets."

Jared is human. He's experienced hesitation, like the rest of us, but has seen too many people's dreams dashed by their inability to get over the hurdles.

THE DIGITAL WHIZ

The final story is about my good friend Jim, with whom I've spent many an enjoyable Saturday morning having cups of steamed milk (neither of us needs caffeine to fuel the conversation) at a local coffeehouse while solving all the problems of the world.

While I'm the researcher, teacher, and author, for almost twenty years my friend has been at the front of the pack when it comes to anything digital, following earlier positions as a frustrated screenwriter, television station account executive, sales manager, and successful author. I'm high energy, but he's even more intense, and I always tell him that after a couple of hours with him I feel like I need a nap.

He started in sales for one of the first big Internet portals and eventually became a VP and the national sales manager. He made a lot of money, even though it wasn't the money as much as the challenges that he loved.

Jim has always been one of the most entrepreneurial guys I've ever known, and when it appeared his role was becoming same old, same old, he started thinking about giving up the cushy job and starting a consulting company teaching digital start-ups how to ramp up the sales of their online advertising. He had a young family to support and a big mortgage on a new home, and he thought about what might happen if things didn't work out. Weighing the risks of starting a new venture or riding things out at a company that was becoming increasingly bureaucratic, he concluded that he was young and talented with a special set of skills that would always be in demand, so he pulled the pin.

Finding clients was never a problem. Jim had a great reputation for being visionary and making things happen, and he always delivered the results he had promised. He was spending a few days each month with a number of companies building their sales and marketing plans and getting them up and running when he received a call from a new social media startup.

They wanted Jim to join them full-time, which meant giving up the other clients in his practice, but in return they offered him big money, a generous number of stock options, and the chance to really make a difference. Jim found the youthful team at the start-up exciting, and after a lot of romancing by the company he didn't hesitate to give it a go.

One of his first responsibilities was to put together an advertising revenue forecast. While simultaneously assembling a team of people, he studiously put together an exacting yet very optimistic set of numbers.

When he presented the numbers to the rest of the senior leadership team, a top executive simply said, "The numbers aren't high enough; go back and make them higher."

Jim played with the numbers some more, but during their next meeting the top executive said, "They still aren't high enough; make them even higher," at which point Jim protested. "If I make them any higher I'll be lying."

"Do whatever you need to do to put together some numbers that give me a story to tell!" responded the exasperated executive, clearly beginning to lose his patience with my friend.

Jim studied the numbers one more time and realized he couldn't hesitate. While he had a great gig with a company he believed would take off, if he put together a set of totally bogus numbers that couldn't be attained he'd be selling his soul and would also be complicit in lying, something he found personally repugnant. He decided that sticking by a guiding principle that had served him well was more important than being party to a lie.

Finally, summoning up his courage, he met with the executive one more time and said, "These are the numbers that can be achieved and delivered. I won't lie and put together a bogus set of numbers just for buzz."

"Well, unless you give me the numbers I want perhaps this company isn't the right place for you," the executive replied.

Jim, a highly principled guy, walked out with his honor intact, quickly revived his highly successful consulting practice, went back to spending a lot of time with his wife and young children and our occasional Saturday morning cup of steamed milk, and almost forgot something important.

Although the company he left didn't come close to hitting the early advertising revenue numbers Jim had promised them, it did prove to be a master at creating buzz, and eventually those stock options he'd almost forgotten turned out to be worth thirty million dollars.

He hadn't sold out, he'd refused to lie, he'd stuck by his guiding principles, and although like most of us he'd hesitated a bit in the end, he did the right thing and was rewarded.

WHAT THEY HAVE IN COMMON

Let me explain the things my friend Jim, my new friend Jared, and banker Ron Nicklaus have in common.

They don't live large, despite being able to. None of them is trying to hit a target number; they're all on a challenging and joy-ridden journey of growth. All of them repeatedly proved themselves able to embrace constant reinvention and change direction as needed.

None of them started with any financial advantage, and they were all forced to do everything frugally. They've all been masters at systems—Jim at teaching companies how to kick-start and maintain digital advertising sales, Jared by having incredible systems for achieving 99.5 percent occupancy in the buildings he owns, and even Ron's River Valley bank has systematized the best way to answer the telephone (I urge you to call one of their branches to find out how).

They all made lots of small bets along the way, and in short, they've followed every lesson in this book for embracing constant radical change and reinvention.

But the single most important thing they share is that each faced the same fears and hesitation we all face, but they summoned up their courage and took the leap in order to create better tomorrows for themselves and their families.

WHY DO PEOPLE HESITATE?

I'm intrigued by people. I ask a lot of questions and listen intently. I look to see how they react to what I ask. I especially like to hear when they succeed in their chosen endeavor, and I empathize when they fall short. "Only a fool fails to learn from his mistakes," my father used to say. "But if you can learn from the mistakes of others, you can be exceptional." I've made it my business to learn from both.

After twenty years of systematic observation I've decided the most common mistake is for one to get stuck on the "plains of hesitation." The plains of hesitation are a metaphorical place where the best laid plans and good intentions expire. (Recall the epigraph at the beginning of this chapter: "On the plains of hesitation bleach the bones of countless millions who on the dawn of victory paused to rest, and while resting died.") The bones of bookseller Borders Group Inc. are currently bleaching there alongside others such as Wang Laboratories, Arthur Andersen, Polaroid, and innumerable others—all who knew enough to make the right moves but hesitated to do so.

Here are nine reasons I've seen and heard most often as I search to understand why we hesitate:

Why people hesitate to act

- Gotten too comfortable
- Study things to death
- Lack of confidence
- Think the big deal will fly in the window
- Think it's already too late for them
- Fear of losing what they have
- Afraid nobody will pitch in
- Family pressures to not take the risk
- Lack of financial safety net

We Get Too Comfortable

An argument can be made that up until the past decade, if someone simply repeated what they'd done before, stayed under the radar, and didn't call attention to themselves, they could hope to achieve the same or similar results in the future. When business results were more easily predicted, it was understandable that people became comfortable and complacent, lulling themselves into believing that life was good and would always be the same. Things don't work that way any longer, and anyone who thinks they do is either delusional or is sitting out the digital revolution.

Today, every business, including yours, is being observed and studied by others who want your revenues. The world operates with such speed that as soon as potential competitors sniff out the fact that another business is doing well and they believe there's a buck to be made they'll be all over it like a cheap suit—probably with greater resources to exploit it or greater efficiencies to do things cheaper. Each day, you publish your best ideas for the world to see whether you know it or not.

The other peril in allowing oneself to become comfortable is the disconnect it causes between the one who is comfortable and those members of the team or workforce who aren't.

Almost without exception the people who report to or work for you want to have better tomorrows for themselves and their families. They want to be challenged, earn more money, advance, grow, and be part of a winning team. The moment they realize that the boss is comfortable and there won't be opportunities for them, they'll emotionally check out and begin seeking other opportunities.

Eventually, when the good people leave, the once-comfortable owner, boss, or manager will find herself in a scramble to put the pieces together alone or with a new and inexperienced bunch of people. She'll also probably find herself in competition with the good people who left because she got comfortable.

Are you hesitant to embrace change and reinvention because you're comfortable? There's no place in business for anyone who wants to be comfortable or complacent. If your desire to be comfortable is greater than your need to embrace change, it's probably time to call it a day, wrap things up, and put the business into hungry hands.

We Study Things to Death

A popular saying is, "Change for change's sake is stupid." As a result of the research for this book, I no longer subscribe to that school of thought. My aha moment on the subject came when Dan DiMicco, CEO of Nucor Corporation, told me that the company implements every suggestion put forth by the company's workers to increase productivity. "We'll try anything," he said, "and if it works we'll get word out to all the other plants, and if it doesn't work we abandon it without any criticism or punishment of the person who suggested it." Imagine what a culture of quick decision making at every level of the organization is created when constant change is embraced and celebrated.

All of the companies and people we studied have another decided advantage when it comes to making decisions: They possess a set of firmly entrenched guiding principles that are well known to everyone within the company. When they have to make a decision, the only question that needs to be answered is, "Does this fit our guiding principles?"

Charles Schwab, the brokerage and investment company I first wrote about a decade ago in *It's Not the Big That Eat the Small . . . It's the Fast That Eat the Slow,* has since tripled in size and grown into a company whose ten million clients entrust the firm with more than

$1.8 trillion. At Schwab, making decisions, including big ones, is guided by answering the following questions about any choice.

Charles Schwab's Guiding Principles

▶ Does it scale our business to make financial services more accessible to all?

▶ Does it innovate with new products and tools that put financial fitness within reach for every investor?

▶ Does it inform and empower investors, because we believe that the best investor is a knowledgeable one?

▶ Does it view our business through clients' eyes?

▶ Does it reinvent our business?

▶ We will risk short-term revenue loss to do the right thing for the long term.

▶ Does it respect our fellow employees and the spirit of teamwork?

By the time the leaders at Charles Schwab have answered the preceding questions, a decision has been made. Unlike in so many other companies, there are no endless meetings, no wringing of hands, no waiting for every self-important wannabe to weigh in with his or her two cents, and no need to start a long, drawn-out process to get a decision made.

Do you and your company have a set of guiding principles? Does everyone know them and use them to make all the decisions that must be made? Having a firmly entrenched set of guiding principles will allow you to skip the excessive studying and get over any hesitation you might have.

Lack of Confidence

A lack of confidence exists in people and organizations that fear criticism, feel they're inferior, lack assertiveness, and/or strive for perfection. The people you've read about in this book have dealt with the lack of confidence that everyone experiences from time to time, by doing the following:

▶ They constantly build their self-esteem and confidence by making lots of small bets and celebrating their wins, which has empowered them to make larger bets and bigger decisions.

▶ They view failure not as a fatal character flaw but as a learning experience that will make their next decision or attempt even better.

▶ They spend time with positive, like-minded people and rid themselves and their organizations of negative people and influences.

▶ They view perfection as the enemy of the good and would rather be good or very good at a number of things than strive for perfection and never get their initiative off the ground.

Confidence comes from winning, and winning only happens when you set your hesitation aside and get in the game.

We Think the Big Deal Will Fly in the Window

During the time I owned radio stations, an average salesperson sold about $30,000 in advertising each month, earning about $75,000 annually at a 20 percent commission, a good income at the time.

If he consistently did that for a few years, he could become a team leader and make about $125,000 annually, eventually earning $150,000-plus as a sales manager.

One of the most talented salespeople I ever hired was a young, handsome guy from the East Coast named Peter. He had more charm and natural ability to connect with people than anyone I'd ever met, and he seemingly possessed all the skills required for the job—he was smart and aggressive and believed in bringing true value to his clients. I remember thinking that he'd go far.

While the other salespeople were out building a base and courting clients who'd spend a few thousand dollars monthly for an effective advertising program, Peter was always trying to do the two-hundred-thousand to three-hundred-thousand-dollar deal. Despite hours of training, counseling, and mentoring, he couldn't let go of chasing the impossible big deals and remained completely convinced he'd be all set once they started flying in the window. Unfortunately, he failed miserably.

Over the next couple of decades I'd occasionally hear about Peter, and it was always the same story. He was working on a big deal that was just about to happen and then he'd be all set. Tragically, he lost it all, including his home, his family, and any sense of self-esteem, and eventually became a dark and cynical figure given to drunken telephone rants directed at the people he believed had kept him from scoring the big deals.

Peter was blinded by greed and didn't want to be bothered building a solid base of business in order to provide security for himself and his family. Like someone addicted to gambling, he only wanted the immediate gratification of the big payoff.

A lot of people and companies are like Peter. They chase the big deal or wait for it to fly in the window.

People and companies who embrace change and reinvention aren't held hostage by the hesitation that comes with waiting for the next big deal. When big deals happen they're as joyous as the next guy, but they know their odds of being the beneficiary of the occasional big deal are greatly increased by doing loads of small deals, learning from each, and constantly incrementally increasing their business.

We Think It's Already Too Late

Mary Kay Ash was in her late forties and had spent more than twenty-five years in the direct-selling business. She was serving as a company's national training director when yet another man she had trained was promoted above her at twice her annual salary.

Remembering the words of her mother, who had constantly told her, "You can do it, Mary Kay; you can do it," she decided that the sweetest revenge was success, so she took her five thousand dollars in life savings and enlisted her twenty-year-old son, Richard, to help her build Beauty by Mary Kay (now Mary Kay Inc.).

Today Mary Kay cosmetics are sold by an army of more than two million direct-sales representatives in forty nations, and the company generates nearly three billion in annual sales.

Harland "Colonel" Sanders started Kentucky Fried Chicken when he was sixty-five years old and it went on to become the most successful franchise operation in the world (at the time). The backstory that most people don't know is that he'd spent twenty-five years owning a gas station in North Corbin, Kentucky, developing his pressure-frying method and selling homemade chicken dinners to his customers.

Eventually, Sanders built a highly successful restaurant, but none of us would have ever heard of him if the government hadn't built I-75, which directed traffic away from his business. Determined to make lemonade out of lemons, he sold the restaurant and began traveling the country and franchising the company, and the rest is a wonderful bit of history.

But author Harry Bernstein takes the cake for believing it's never too late to start. He published a short story when he was in his early twenties, but it wasn't until his wife of sixty-seven years passed away that he began penning *The Invisible Wall*, the story of his hardscrabble youth in England before emigrating to the U.S. The book became a best-selling hit for Random House when Bernstein was—get ready for this—ninety-six years old.

I'm certain that at some point Mary Kay Ash, Colonel Sanders, and Harry Bernstein considered their age and maybe hesitated. Thankfully, they didn't.

Fear of Losing What We Have

We all wrestle with the fear of losing what we have. On occasion we read about the highly successful venture that was founded by someone maxing out ten credit cards, but those stories are the exception. When you dig a little deeper into those stories you generally find that the one betting it all is someone with nothing to lose and who can walk away from it all if the bet doesn't pay off.

The refrain we constantly heard from the entrepreneurs and leaders during our research was to never bet the ranch but to make lots of small bets, learn from them, and then scale.

If you haven't figured out a way to provide yourself and your family the basics, you won't be of much use to anyone. Smart moves seldom come from desperation. But once you have the level of financial security that makes you comfortable, stop hesitating and bet away.

Fear That Nobody Will Pitch In

During the past decade I've studied hundreds of thousands of companies and talked to tens of thousands of people, and prior to that I employed thousands. Two observations sum up everything I've learned from those experiences: Everybody wants a better tomorrow and everyone wants to be part of a winning team.

Ask almost anyone about their best memories aside from family, and chances are very good they're going to tell you about a winning team they were on, a military unit they served in, a band they played in, a business upstart that really worked out, or a time they were made to feel very special.

People are willing to pitch in, help out, and be part of something bigger than themselves. The task of the person leading the effort is to present his or her idea for growth or change in a way that makes sense and has a noble purpose attached to it, one in which people can see they'd be recognized for their contributions and maybe even have some fun. If you're capable of doing those things there's no need to hesitate and worry if people will pitch in. You'll have all the help you need.

Family Pressures to Not Take the Risk

My mother has a sweatshirt that reads, "Our Family Puts the FUN in Dysfunctional!" and she wears it proudly. Despite everyone's best efforts to the contrary, most families are so riddled with memories, hurt, pain, and slights (real and imagined) that they tend to be kind of weird.

In some instances family members have vivid recollections of failure and don't want others to face the same pain they've experienced.

So if Uncle Frank lost the house and ended up mired in poverty because he bet everything on a deal that went bad, it's understandable that Mom might have a bad recollection about someone who took a chance and lost.

In other cases there's a lack of understanding because of a lack of experience. If two parents have never been away from their small hometown, it's understandable that they might discourage their daughter from moving to the big city and pursuing her dream.

There are lots of other emotions at play in families as well. Sometimes the pressure not to take a chance is based on jealousy: "Well, the family business has always been good enough for everyone else." And sometimes it's based on selfishness: "Well, I guess it's okay if I never get to see my grandchildren again."

The best advice I can offer on dealing with mothers, fathers, sisters, and brothers pressuring people not to take any chances is as follows: Move two thousand miles away, build your own life, visit twice a year, call frequently, love them, and forgive them.

Lack of a Financial Safety Net

There is no magic number for determining the financial safety net someone requires.

Everyone's need for a safety net is different. Someone in his twenties without any obligations or worries about where the next dollar will come from will have far different needs for financial safety than someone in his thirties with two small kids and a mortgage. Similarly, someone in his forties with the dream of a paid-off mortgage and the kids out of the house about to happen will have different needs than someone in his fifties or sixties with everything paid off.

When the lack of a financial safety net is causing the hesitation that's preventing change and growth from occurring, it's clearly an issue, and everyone has to determine their own tolerance for risk and what size safety net they need.

The important thing is that the issue is discussed and agreed upon before a course of action is undertaken. There's nothing worse than a spouse emptying the family bank accounts without letting others know that he is funding his dream.

A LAST WORD OF ADVICE

An ancient Chinese proverb says, "A man must sit in chair with his mouth open for awfully long time before a roasted duck flies in."

If you have made it this far, you must agree with the premise that organizations need to grow and that the only way to accomplish continual growth is by embracing constant change in order to stay ahead of your customers. I'm confident you now have the guiding principles, the unconventional wisdom, the cutting-edge tactics, and the stories that will help you get that done.

Don't hesitate.

Here's to embracing constant change and reinvention.

ACKNOWLEDGMENTS

The original idea for *The Reinventors* wasn't mine.

While wrestling with several possible subjects that I might want to research and write about, I had one of my frequent phone conversations with Bruce Ritter, my close friend and investment adviser. Generally we argue about politics, but that day we were talking about the need to constantly remain relevant. Only seconds after we'd finished our conversation he called back and said, "Your next book needs to be about reinvention. Good-bye." Then he proceeded to hound me daily with evidence of why the book needed to be written.

Adrian Zackheim, my publisher, is widely acknowledged as being the best business and leadership publisher in the industry. He has an uncanny ability to know what will work and what won't. This book required only a fifteen-minute meeting in his office and a deal was done the next day. This is my fifth book with him; I'm grateful he continues to take chances with me, and I hope there will be many more books to come.

For the initial research I called on the resources of Steve McIntosh, of Research on Demand, in Santa Barbara, California, and Beijing; and Prakash Idnani, in Madras, India. For the first time ever I used my Web site and social media to invite submissions of possible candidates. In total more than twenty-two thousand candidate companies were considered.

There was an overwhelming amount of data to digest and sort out, and I called on Laurence Haughton, my coauthor on *It's Not the Big That Eat the Small . . . It's the Fast That Eat the Slow* and the author of *It's Not What You Say . . . It's What You Do.* He's worked for me and with me for more than twenty years, and I thoroughly enjoyed having someone to assist me with the research and bounce ideas off of. I anxiously await my next project with him. He's the best!

There's a small team around me that makes everything work so that I have the time to research and write my books. They include Caryn Shehi, who manages not only my speeches but every aspect of my business life; Christopher DiSalvio, who does the bookkeeping and looks after our home in California; and Gene and Judy Nagel, who manage our beloved lodge in Michigan's rugged and beautiful Upper Peninsula. Bill Deane is the digital wizard who keeps us all connected, and Mark Powell handles the travel and gets me back and forth to all the places I need to be. Ana Baradello and Zamil Sadiq teach me Spanish and the viola and bring unbridled joy to my life.

Emily Angell was the editor on the book and did a terrific job. She worked me harder than any other editor with whom I've worked. It was a pleasure to work with her—give me a young, plugged-in, challenging editor anytime. As always I extend heartfelt gratitude to the entire team at Portfolio for all their help, including Will Weisser, the head of marketing; Allison McLean, the head of publicity; and Jacquelynn Burke, the publicist for this book.

Finally, I thank the companies and leaders featured in the book. When an author calls and says, "I want to write about you and your company," it takes an amazing leap of faith to say yes and open your life and company to a third party's endless questions and inspection. Eventually great leaders and companies agree to be featured because they understand they have an obligation to help other entrepreneurs and leaders.

If you enjoy and learn from *The Reinventors* it's because of the efforts of the people previously listed. Hopefully, by the time you read this we'll all be together again working on another book for you.

By George, we've survived and finished another one!

INDEX

OTHER BOOKS BY JASON JENNINGS

THINK BIG, ACT SMALL
How America's Best Performing Companies
Keep the Start-up Spirit Alive
(New York: Portfolio, 2005, 2012)

Think Big, Act Small shares the secrets of nine companies who have done something one hundred thousand other companies haven't: They've grown their revenues and profits by 10 percent or more for fifteen consecutive years.

Getting inside these quiet superstars, Jennings and his team questioned the leaders, workers, and customers and uncovered an astonishingly simple precept—they all think big but act small—and from there built their road maps to astoundingly consistent, profitable growth.

Think Big, Act Small is teeming with unforgettable stories, brilliant lessons, and a test that helps you evaluate where you are today compared with the top-performing companies in the world. No matter what size you are or what industry you are in, you will benefit from this book.

THE TEN BUILDING BLOCKS OF
THINKING BIG AND ACTING SMALL

DOWN TO EARTH

KEEP YOUR HANDS DIRTY (SAS INSTITUTE)

SHORT TERM GOALS AND LONG TERM
HORIZONS (SONIC)

LET GO (CABELA'S)

HAVE EVERYONE THINK AND ACT LIKE THE OWNER
(KOCH INDUSTRIES)

HIT THE GROUND RUNNING
A Manual for New Leaders
(New York: Portfolio, 2009)

In *Hit the Ground Running*, Jennings identifies the nine top performing new CEOs of the Fortune 1000 class of 2001–2008. Their stories give you a front-row seat to learning how each quickly pulled together their teams, implemented their strategies, and hit the ground running—doubling revenues, tripling earnings, and making everyone proud that these CEOs were chosen to lead.

These powerful case studies include: Goodrich Corporation (CEO Marshall Larsen), Allegheny Technologies (CEO L. Patrick Hassey), Mohawk Industries (CEO Jeff Lorberbaum), Questar Corporation (CEO Keith Rattie), the Hanover Insurance Group (CEO Frederick Eppinger), J.M. Smucker Company (co-CEOs Tim and Richard Smucker), Staples (CEO Ron Sargent), Humana (CEO Michael McCallister), and Harris Corporation (CEO Howard Lance).

The Ten Rules in
Hit the Ground Running

You Will Reap What You Sow
Gain Belief
Ask for Help
Find, Keep, and Grow the Right People
See Through the Fog
Drive a Stake in the Ground
Simplify Everything
Be Accountable
Cultivate a Fierce Sense of Urgency
Be a Fish out of Water

Hit the Ground Running is available from Portfolio (an imprint of Penguin Group USA).

LESS IS MORE
How Great Companies Use Productivity as a Competitive Tool in Business
(New York: Portfolio, 2002)

The best-selling *Less Is More* identifies the most productive companies on the planet based on the criteria of revenue, cash flow, return on invested capital, and return on equity *per employee per year.*

The companies written about in the book include: Nucor Corporation, World Savings, Yellow Transportation, IKEA, Lantec (a manufacturing company in Louisville, Kentucky), SRC Holdings, the Warehouse (a New Zealand and Australian chain of discount stores), and Ryanair (Europe's largest discount airline).

KEY FINDINGS

Focus
Productive companies all have a big objective
The culture is the strategy
Streamline
Tell the truth
Simplify everything
Get rid of the wrong managers and execs fast
No mass layoffs
WTGBRFDT?
The real financial drivers
Systematize everything
Continuous improvement
Compensation
Digitize
The plug-in myth
Technology does not create a competitive advantage
Motivate
Keeping everyone on the same page
People are naturally motivated, so remove barriers of frustration
Embody
A lean spirit
Leadership traits:
    long-term focus
    embrace simplicity
    high moral fiber
    humility
    coach leadership
    reject bureaucracy
    believe in others; trust
    institutionalize leadership

Less Is More is available from Portfolio (an imprint of Penguin Group USA) in both hardcover and paperback editions.